# BELSIZE
## Remembered

# About this Book

Research for this collection of memories of Belsize Park commenced in January 2012, and as a long time resident of the area it has been an honour to spearhead this project. These accounts from the 20th century were gathered over five years by advertising in local newspapers, drop-in sessions at the Belsize Community Library, and by word of mouth. Additionally, some of the reminiscences are drawn from the documentary film *The Belsize Story*.

People were generous with their personal stories from their lives in Belsize Park. Everyone emphasised how lucky they were to have grown up here, to have come to live in the area, or simply to have passed through, making it their home at one time or another.

Contributions were received mostly in written form, although a few were obtained through recorded interviews. The interviews were transcribed verbatim, and together with the written pieces they were respectfully edited and assembled, taking into consideration their relationship to Belsize Park and their general interest. The authors have given consent for their work to be published in this book. We received almost a hundred submissions in total.

Historical and contemporary images of Belsize Park were selected by David Percy from his archive and ingeniously combined with the texts.

We are grateful to all those who have contributed to these memories of Belsize. No doubt it was a pleasurable experience for each contributor to go back and revisit his or her past. It certainly has been a pleasure to compile these memoirs and get to know some of the authors.

**Ranee Barr**

# BELSIZE Remembered

## MEMORIES OF BELSIZE PARK

Compiled by Ranee Barr
and David S Percy

Edited by F Peter Woodford

λ
Aulis Publishers
London

# BELSIZE Remembered
## MEMORIES OF BELSIZE PARK

Compiled by Ranee Barr
and David S Percy

Edited by F Peter Woodford

Photographs by David S Percy
except where otherwise stated

Archive images are digitally restored

Cover illustration by Paul McBride

Aulis Publishers
1 Belsize Avenue
London NW3 4BL UK
belsizevillage.co.uk

British Library Cataloguing-in-Publication Data
A catalogue record of this book is available from the British Library

© Aulis Publishers 2017
Reprinted 2018

ISBN 978-1-898541-08-0

Copyright in the individual accounts belongs to the respective authors;
they may not be reproduced without the permission of both author and publisher

Printed and bound by SRP Ltd Exeter UK

# Contents

| | |
|---|---|
| Foreword | vi |
| Preface and Acknowledgements | vii |
| A Brief History of Belsize | ix |
| The Reminiscences | 1 |
| Map of Belsize Conservation Areas | 179 |
| The Belsize Residents' Association | 182 |
| Notable Former Residents | 184 |
| Author Index | 185 |
| Individual Donors | 186 |
| Index | 187 |
| Archive Image Sources | 192 |

# Foreword
## *Sir Derek Jacobi*

It was a coincidence that brought me to live in Belsize Park. During the making of the television series *I, Claudius* I regularly visited the writer of the script (Jack Pulman) at his house in Belsize Park. I came to love the house and the area so much that when he died I bought the house from his widow. I was told that the previous owner had been the famous performer Leslie Hutchinson known as 'Hutch'. So as you can see the house has been lived in by an artist of one form or another. And I can understand why.

The area of Belsize exudes a certain vibrancy, understated yet captivating with its quality of light and space. It is so near the West End, yet one gets the feeling of being somewhere remote. With its several 'villages' it has a unique rural/metropolitan aura.

Belsize is of course fortunate to have three green spaces within close proximity – Primrose Hill and Regent's Park on one end, and Hampstead Heath in the opposite direction. This in itself is exceptional. As I am a devoted dog owner the area is a dog's delight.

Being a man of the theatre, I can be in the West End in fifteen minutes. But when I return I feel as though I have come to a home in a village. The tranquillity is complete. Belsize has long been home to thespians and it is no wonder!

Other things I like about Belsize are its wide pavements, and everywhere one looks it is lush and green. Plus, of course, the good mix of architecture: be it terraced, semi-detached or blocks or discreet modern additions, they all sit comfortably next to each other: the Victorian, Edwardian, Art Deco and the modern.

I started my acting career in a library in the East End aged six. Libraries became part of my growing up, and I cannot stress enough their importance. I have visited the dear little Belsize Library in Antrim Road several times and love it.

Sir Derek Jacobi

*Photo: Stuart Wilson/Getty*

# Preface and Acknowledgements

The publication *Belsize Remembered* is a collection of reminiscences of life past and present in Belsize Park. It was inspired by the popular 2001 publication *Primrose Hill Remembered*.

Ranee Barr has led the Belsize Reminiscence Project from the outset and steered it through all stages of development with advice and support of Gene Adams and Myra Newman.

Following the successful exhibition 'Belsize in View' curated by local film-maker/photographer David S Percy at Burgh House & Hampstead Museum in the spring of 2016, it was suggested that this project should combine the collected memories with a selection of recent photographs taken in and around Belsize Park.

We are immensely grateful to all those who have contributed by revisiting their past and recording their memories of this wonderful part of London for future generations.

Publication of this 2018 reprint has been made possible through the generous assistance of the primary sponsors, Knight Frank Belsize Park Estate Agents. Thanks also to the original sponsors, Heywoods Estate Agents and XUL Architecture.

The project is also supported by Belsize Conservation Area Advisory Committee, Camden Local Studies and Archives Centre, Burgh House & Hampstead Museum, Friends of the Belsize Community Library, and many individual donors (p186).

Grateful thanks to all the sponsors, donors and supporters of this project

Project supported by

Belsize Conservation Area Advisory Committee

Camden Local Studies and Archives Centre

Belsize House: *View of a House and its Estate in Belsize, Middlesex* 1696 Jan Siberechts, *Tate Images*
the second of four incarnations of Belsize House (1496, 1663, 1745 and 1812)

# A Brief History of Belsize

Belsize was not always as it is today – the developers didn't arrive until the early 19th century. For centuries it was just rolling countryside, mostly farmland, trees and lakes with only a handful of grand houses and their extensive grounds.

Originally, Belsize was part of Hampstead. Records start as early as 986 when King Ethelred the Unready granted the Manor of Hampstead to the Abbot and Benedictine Monks of St Peter's, Westminster. It was about 2,100 acres and is referred to in the Domesday Book. At the end of the 12th century, the Abbot separated out the Belsize estate of 230 acres from the Manor of Hampstead, and gave it to his Prior.

Then, between 1536 and 1541, Henry VIII dissolved all the monasteries and grabbed their lands. He seized the entire Manor of Hampstead, including Belsize. But within a few years, the King had a change of heart. The Belsize estate was handed to Dr. Thomas Thirlby who was Bishop of Westminster in the newly-founded Church of England. This bishopric was short-lived, and when it expired in 1550, the estate was taken over by the Dean and Chapter of Westminster.

The major part of Hampstead was given to the courtier and landowner Sir Thomas Wroth. His grandson sold the manor to Sir Baptist Hicks in 1620, and Lordship of the Manor remains in private hands to this day, although his rights are now purely nominal. Belsize continued as a separate entity in the possession of the Dean and Chapter of Westminster, though leased to a succession of private persons.

**Belsize House**

Belsize House at the centre of the estate was a grand country house with extensive grounds (see picture opposite) in a prime location outside London for hundreds of years. There was nothing to interrupt the view to Westminster Abbey apart from Primrose Hill in the middle distance. The surrounding area was arable land, with market gardens for vegetables and pasture supplying feed for London's many horses. The Belsize estate obtained most of its own food from Belsize Farm, nearby on Belsize Lane.

A map of Belsize was prepared in 1679 by William Gent, illustrating the position of the Manor House and its estate. In order to demonstrate to the French that London was larger than Paris, in the mid 1700s, the cartographer John Rocque was commissioned to create a plan of London and the surrounding areas. This mapping project turned out to be a work of art.

We can trace Belsize House back to at least 1496 at the dawn of the Tudor period, when the Abbey ordered 400,000 bricks for its construction. The property was rebuilt and improved many times during the centuries that followed. There were at least four successive buildings, all called Belsize House.

It was probably in 1663 that one of the richest men in England, Colonel Daniel O'Neil, began building a mansion for his wife, Katherine, the Countess of Chesterfield (by a previous marriage). The house looked very handsome in its setting with a tree-lined driveway in the foreground leading off the London Road at Haverstock Hill. Primrose Hill is clearly visible, and St Peter's Abbey in Westminster is there in the central distance.

The house itself had a generous courtyard and was surrounded by extensive walled gardens. The grand driveway leading to the house and grounds was to become today's Belsize Avenue.

The diarists Sir John Evelyn and Samuel Pepys both recorded visits to the estate. Pepys called on Lord Wotton in 1668, and this is his diary entry for the 17th of August:

"…Went and saw the Lord Wotton's house and garden, which is wonderfull fine: too good for the house the gardens are, being, indeed, the most noble that ever I saw." >

The second Belsize House (garden front) with extended wings and added central tower, *archive wood engraving*

Belsize House, 1745 version
*engraving from around 1800*

Part of John Rocque's 1746 map of London centred on Belsize House and grounds

The gardens were said to be on a par with other great gardens in London such as New Spring Garden – later called Vauxhall Gardens.

Then the property was sub-let to the writer Charles Povey, who decided to open Belsize House and gardens to the public, with a private chapel available for marriages. Deer hunting was introduced to the park – all part of the pleasure activities of Belsize House. Some 16 years later, the occupant was James Howell, known as the Welsh Ambassador. The *Daily Post* of 1720, founded by Daniel Defoe stated that the "ancient and noble house" had been fitted up for entertainment during the summer season, and was to be opened with "Dancing and Music." Visitors could fish or hunt in the grounds, dine on the best food, enjoy fine wines, and dance in the lavish ballroom.

The following August, the *Daily Post* reported: >

"One hundred coaches will stand in the square of the house", and "Twelve men will continue to guard the road every night 'till the last of the company are gone."

A year later in 1721, the Prince and Princess of Wales dined at Belsize House. It became very much the place to be seen, prompting large numbers of visitors to sample the delights of Belsize. But within a year, the greed of the visitors and their goings on got completely out of hand, with deteriorating, unseemly behaviour.

There was public outrage over these unacceptable activities. And the large numbers of visitors caused frequent traffic jams on the main carriageway from Haverstock Hill, so the house was closed in 1745. But not for long! After a year or so Belsize House had been rebuilt and became a residence again, this time a Georgian-style mansion, positioned facing London.

Belsize House returned to normality and slowly regained its respectability. Just over 50 years later, the house was occupied for a while by the prominent politician, later prime minister, Spencer Perceval. He is chiefly remembered as the only British Prime Minister ever to have been assassinated – he was shot in the lobby of the House of Commons in 1812. Nearby Perceval Avenue is named after him.

**The first housing developments**
There were four farms in the area in the 1800s: Belsize Farm, Upper Chalcots Farm, Lower Chalcots Farm or Chalk Farm, and South End Farm, at South End Green.

An 1807 act of parliament empowered distant descendants of the Countess of Chesterfield (who still held leases) to sub-lease plots for development. The Dean and Chapter of Westminster continued to own the land, and they granted eight separate leases in 1808. New building in Belsize got underway. Edward Bliss developed the first plot.

In 1855 a Bloomsbury solicitor, Charles James Palmer, bought the head-lease of Belsize House and decided to demolish it and develop the whole area as an upmarket housing estate. So the first streets of central Belsize were planned out, Daniel Tidey and William Willett & Sons being the primary developers.

In 1876, the part of the London Road leading from Chalk Farm to Pond Street was named Haverstock Hill, after the rising ground up which it climbs.

It is often forgotten that the original Belsize estate also included a considerable area of land east of Haverstock Hill, which extended from the road now named South Hill Park on the slope of Parliament Hill all the way down to what is now Prince of Wales Road. Substantial Victorian houses were built on much of this land, except for the part occupied by market gardens (John Russell Nurseries). Their garden sheds bordered Haverstock Hill through into the 1920s, when the parade of shops and restaurants with flats above was constructed here; the tennis club and courts behind it were preserved.

As families then began to shrink in size, and servants became harder and harder to find, the large houses on both sides of Haverstock Hill and in the former grounds of Belsize House were split up into ever smaller units, and Belsize Park became known as bedsitter land. Greedy landlords allowed the stucco to peel and roofs to leak. Impecunious, formerly well-to-do refugees from Nazi Germany and elsewhere moved in, desperately clinging on to respectability while the area became notoriously shabby.

After World War II and with a gradual rise in prosperity, people began to realise the potential of the substantial, basically sound buildings ranged along wide, tree-lined streets, and set to work restoring them to their former glory. In a few decades Belsize became an elegant, desirable place to live in. Men and women who worked hard to beautify their surroundings alongside others doing likewise seem to have developed a community spirit not so keenly felt in districts that have never gone through darker times.

It seems a good moment (in 2017) to tap into the memories of those who have experienced this heartening period of rejuvenation as well as those who remember the pains and joys of living here in the drearier times. Many of those former residents have moved away. Those who return are astonished at its present appearance. We hope that the reminiscences that follow will capture the flavour of what both newcomers and old hands in the area feel about where they live.

The grand, tree-lined carriageway that originally led to Belsize House, c.1860
this was to become Belsize Avenue, *archive*

Belsize Avenue, 2013

Belsize Park

# In a Belsize Bookshop
## *Frances Pinter*

My very first visit to Belsize many years ago took me to Don Woodford's bookshop on Haverstock Hill. There I found a little old lady telling off the bookseller, saying that he should get rid of a table full of books by Carl Jung. Bewildered, the bookseller asked "Why?"

The little old lady said, "My good friend Thomas Mann lived right next door to Carl Jung, and knew him perfectly well, yet when we went walking on Sundays Jung would walk right by us and not even say hello. What's more, Mrs Jung habitually did her vacuum cleaning every day when Thomas Mann took his nap, and refused to change this even when Mrs Mann wrote to Mrs Jung asking her to do it at a different time. And yet you have a table full of books by this terrible man!"

When I overheard this conversation I knew I had to come and live in Belsize Park.

Odeon cinema, Haverstock Hill 1937, *RIBA archive*

ARTISTS OF ALL KINDS

# Architects in Belsize
## *Su Rogers*

I lived with my first husband Richard Rogers at No.18 Belsize Grove, between 1964 and 1972. Two of my sons were born there.

Many architects lived in Belsize Park at that time: James Stirling, Léon Krier, David Shalev and Eldred Evans, Rick Mather, Georgie Wolton to name a few of the better-known ones. I think that what architects liked about Belsize was the scale and quality of the architecture. The houses are very grand, with beautiful rooms featuring tall ceilings and large bay windows. We all lived in flats, rather than occupying the whole house, and enjoyed the lateral space. The main shopping hub was then, as it is now, Haverstock Hill. I do not remember there being any good restaurants in those days, nor Daunt Books. There were specialist shops, good greengrocers and the Odeon cinema, but no fish and chips shop and it was not all that useful for feeding a growing family on a limited budget.

There was a general feeling that Hampstead higher up the hill was more upmarket and chic, although personally I would never have wanted to live in Hampstead with its cosy cottages and smug atmosphere! We liked the anonymity of Belsize Park. With some exceptions, Belsize Park was then not so much a family area, but more of a bed-sitter area, with many single and older people. There was a nice park on Antrim Road where I used to take the children and meet other families.

We had our office, Team 4 Architects, in the first floor flat in Hampstead Hill Gardens, which is at the extreme northerly edge of Belsize.

No.18 Belsize Grove

BELSIZE Remembered

# Architect Anne Robinson
## *Anthea Ionides Goldsmith*

On the north side of Belsize Lane, where Village Close is now located, there was just open land extending from the bottom of the large gardens of the detached houses in Lyndhurst Gardens.

My mother Anne Ionides Robinson was an architect and worked at Cluttons 5 Great College Street in Westminster. Cluttons looked after Church property with two departments: Town and Country. She worked in the Town Department. In those days it was called the Ecclesiastical Commission (now Church Commissioners).

Belsize Lane c.1950, *archive*

Village Close (north side) in 2016

In the 1950s my mother was asked to come up with a specification for the site, now Village Close. She replied that she considered two large houses to be inappropriate on the site, as at the time many of the large houses in Belsize Park were being divided into flats. It was smaller properties that were needed. So they asked her to devise a plan she thought would be suitable.

Thus Village Close came into being. I remember that the powers that be wanted each house to have a garage. She refused to break down that wall, and have the cars coming out into Belsize Lane, which was a bit of a rat run. It would also mean felling mature trees. As a result it was arranged that the garages would be built on the other side of the road, behind the pub. The first occupants moved into the houses in 1960.

When she was a child my mother lived at East Heath Lodge and went to King Alfred School which was then in Ellerdale Road. She then went to the Architectural Association (AA) in Bedford Square and became the first woman FRIBA. During the war she worked for Hornsey Borough Council with an office in the Town Hall, Crouch End.

My father was killed in the war, so she was a widow for 16 years. Then she married again, and the new couple moved into No.2 Village Close!

ARTISTS OF ALL KINDS

Belsize Lane 1842, *archive*

BELSIZE Remembered

# Two Authors
## Anna Reiner and Eva Ibbotson

In 2000 an English translation of the novel *Manja* by Anna Gmeyner (alias Anna Reiner) was about to be published by Nicola Beauman's publishing company Persephone Books, with an introduction by Anna's daughter Eva Ibbotson. Jane Wright of the *Ham&High* interviewed Eva, by this time 79 years old.

Mother and daughter arrived in Belsize Park in 1935 when Eva was 9. "I remember our nice, quiet flat in Belsize Park Gardens, where we moved from Belsize Grove. I recall her religiously tapping away at *Manja* there." (Manja is the name of the Polish girl who is the heroine of the story, although the novel [in German, but now available in English translation] is set in the Germany of the 1920s and 30s.)

"[Belsize's] streets abounded with Jewish doctors and lawyers and schoolchildren; with communists and social democrats, with actors and writers and bankers of no particular political persuasion who had spoken out about the Nazis. This band of exiles had been deprived in a few years of the certainty of centuries. The war had not yet come, but these refugees saw its necessity as the British could not yet do. They used their humour to keep the terror and desolation at bay, but it was always there."

Eva's preface to *Manja* is itself a literary work, elegantly unfolding Anna's story. She was a typical product of prosperous, cultured, intellectual bourgeois Viennese Jews. She had been a successful playwright, poet and librettist in Berlin, collaborating with Bertolt Brecht and Hanns Eisler and in Paris with Pabst. In Paris she fell in love with and married a Russian Jewish exile, who fortunately for them both thought Paris was for single gentlemen, whereas London was for married ones. This eventually saved both their lives, as London is where he brought them both.

Eva herself married out of the Jewish faith and moved away from London, but nevertheless produced in 1993 a novel (in English), *The Morning Gift*, about émigrés in Belsize Park, which has also been republished by Persephone Books. Like *Manja*, it is still in print, even available on Kindle. Eva Ibbotson produced more books for adults and children for which she received many awards.

"In *The Morning Gift* I described a lot of sad refugees constantly walking up and down Haverstock Hill to Hampstead Town Hall, hoping for news of refugee relatives and greeting each other with 'Good morning, Herr Doktor'. I learned about having a stiff upper lip in Belsize Library in Antrim Road, where I read all the schoolgirl stories of Angela Brazil. The Willow Café in *The Morning Gift* was actually the Cosmo in Finchley Road, which was taken over by the refugees [p58]. The artist Feliks Topolski did the murals and it served central European food and smelled of red cabbage.

"An English butcher on Haverstock Hill had to adapt to a lot of old ladies suddenly looking for Wiener schnitzel. It's not at all the same as veal steak, but the butcher did his best, beating the steak constantly to get it thinner and thinner. The local shops were also slowly colonised by pickles and gherkins.

"My memories of the period are not entirely happy. My mother's sister committed suicide by jumping out of a second-floor window, after her fiancé broke off their engagement when he discovered she was Jewish."

Eva lived in Belsize Park for five years, until the war broke out and she moved to the Berkshire countryside. "When war broke out a lot of poor refugees who had already fled the Nazis were then scooped up off the streets of London as enemy aliens and taken to be interned on the Isle of Man."

After she left, Eva Ibbotson didn't set foot in Belsize Park for decades. She considered it shabby in the 1930s. "Now I'm amazed how elegant it's become."

Based on the obituary of Anna Gmeyner by **Jane Wright**
*Camden New Journal*, September 2004

Belsize Park Gardens in 1912

Belsize Park Gardens in 2012 shortly after resurfacing work

BELSIZE Remembered

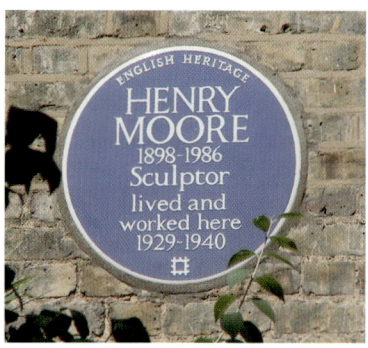

Henry Moore's house, Parkhill Road

*Shelterers in the Tube* 1941
Henry Moore, *Tate*, CC-BY-NC-ND

# Henry Moore and the Blitz of 1940
## *Helen Pollock*

On the 11th of September 1940, Henry Moore and his wife left their house in Parkhill Road to go out to dinner. As their car was temporarily out of action they took the tube.

On the way home the train stopped at every station, where more and more frightened Londoners were taking shelter from the bombing. Moore was shocked, moved and inspired to begin the great series of drawings of the ghostly underground scenes that were to endear him to the British public.

Moore was already Britain's best-known modernist sculptor, but the War Artists' Advisory Committee (a British government agency) which was charged with commissioning Britain's war artists, was not allowed to employ sculptors, presumably because sculpture consumed precious time and material resources. This may explain why Moore turned to drawing as part of his war effort, making frequent trips on foot after that fateful evening to the local Belsize Park Underground station to continue his monumental series.

**The Shelter Drawings**

Henry Moore made notes during the nights he spent in different Underground stations. These served as a basis for the sketches he made the next day.

"One evening after dinner in a restaurant with some friends we returned home by Underground taking the Northern Line to Belsize Park. As a rule I went to town by car and I hadn't been on the tube for ages. For the first time that evening I saw people lying on the platforms at all the stations we stopped at. When we got to Belsize Park we weren't allowed out of the station for an hour because of the bombing. I spent the time looking at the rows of people sleeping on the platforms. I had never seen so many reclining figures, and even the train tunnels seemed to be like the holes in my sculpture. And amid the grim tension, I noticed groups of strangers formed together into intimate groups and children asleep within feet of the passing trains."

John Hedgecoe and Henry Moore, *Henry Moore*
London, Thames Nelson, 1968

Henry Moore in his studio in Parkhill Road
*Henry Moore Foundation*

BELSIZE Remembered

# Alfred East and Belsize Park
## *Toni Huberman*

Sir Alfred East RA (1844-1913) was one of the leading landscape painters of his day, and President of the Royal Society of British Artists (1906). He lived in Belsize Park for over 25 years, initially at No.14 Adamson Road, then at 49 and then 67 Belsize Park, where he died in 1913. The Adamson Road property had only just been built when he moved in during 1885. Later residents included the Camden Town Group painter Robert Bevan [p20].

East painted *A New Neighbourhood* in the mid 1880s. It is of a view from his rear studio window (which would have overlooked the nascent Eton Avenue), depicting a single house under scaffolding being built, with a row of houses in Fellows Road in the distance. It may be the earliest known painting of Eton Avenue. In fact there are four versions of it, one of which is reproduced here.

The watercolour version won the Gold Medal at the Exposition Universelle 1889 in Paris, so it was an important achievement at this stage of his career.

In the early days of Eton Avenue houses had names, not numbers, so it's very difficult to establish which buildings existed. But No.55 has been confirmed as the subject of his painting – it is now the Trevor Roberts School.

*A New Neighbourhood,* Alfred East, c.1885

ARTISTS OF ALL KINDS

# Movie Making in Belsize Park
## Yvonne Deutschman

Belsize Park is a film-maker's dream location. Not only for the wide variety of locations and the pool of local talent as cast and crew but also due to the film-savvy local community willing to support the production in any way they can.

Back in 2011, I directed and produced the feature film *Three To Tango*, a Power of Three production, set in Belsize Park. It is a comedy drama about three women who reunite for a 50th birthday celebration and turn their lives around. The cast was headed by punk rocker/actress Toyah Willcox supported by the crème de la crème of Hampstead's acting sorority, Shirley Ann Field (*Saturday Night, Sunday Morning*), Maggie Nolan (*Goldfinger* and the *Carry On* comedies) and Kara Wilson (theatre performer and artist).

It's amazing how many creative people live in the area. Costume designer Suzi Peters faced a huge challenge in dressing the many female characters on a tight budget. She came up with the ingenious plan of persuading local charity shops to lend clothes with the promise they would be returned dry-cleaned. Camden-based makeup artist Rebecca Wordingham supervised a team of young trainees to ensure that all the ladies looked their most beautiful, with not a hair out of place.

Local film-maker David Percy supplied a professional Sony CineAlta camera for the film shoot and edited the movie in his post-production studio in Belsize Avenue. Such acts of generosity and co-operation were repeated time after time by the whole community. Isolde Hedegaard [p18], wife of celebrated artist Peter Hedegaard, opened up her home in Glenilla Road to serve as the production base.

Over three weeks, cast and crew assembled there every morning at 7am to prepare for the day's filming. It was nothing less than an invasion, with the 30-strong team taking over every room: the vast wardrobe occupied half her living room and the other half was taken up with camera equipment and lights. Catering staff worked from the kitchen. Bedrooms were converted into makeup studios and offices. It was the hub of the production, crucially within walking distance of most of the locations.

Any production designer would die for the locations we had lined up. Local residents agreed to filming in their magnificent homes and gardens. Shopkeepers and restaurant owners opened up their premises for nothing. The much-loved Late Nite Extra newsagent owner Shiraz Alidina, who ran the shop with his wife Tazim for over 35 years in Belsize Village, acted as himself in a series of scenes.

Other settings included the Belsize Village Deli, Oliver's Café, SpringHealth, the Marriott Hotel, the Everyman cinema Hampstead and *The Flask* pub. The tree-lined avenues, the cobbled stone alleyways and landscaped squares provided an elegant backdrop to the action. Belsize Park is as much a character in the film as the actors themselves.

It was a happy and rewarding experience for everyone, how could it not be, working in truly beautiful surroundings within a close-knit community who cherish and actively support the arts. Someone always knew someone who could fulfil the many demands of a making a movie.

Shiraz Alidina

BELSIZE Remembered

Built in 1861, St Peter's original vicarage was located at the eastern end of Belsize Square, *archive*

St Peter's second vicarage was acquired by the Belsize Square Synagogue in 1951

# Opera Singer Mme Zwingli
## *Veronica Jupp Veasey*

As a young child in the 1950s living in my father's vicarage that had just been built in Belsize Square, with its rather haphazard garden he had created at the front, I remember an old Swiss lady, Madame Zwingli. She had been an opera singer, a prima donna, in Edinburgh before the war. Passers by stopped to speak to my father over the fence and so did this lady one day. She asked my father if she could have some berries from the wild elder trees that grew in one corner of our garden, and my father asked if I could visit her for French conversation. I sat in Mme Zwingli's small bed-sitting room and listened while she talked. I could hardly say a word in French but I understood most of what she said. She told me about her glory days when she would sing and then stay awake for hours afterwards, full of excitement.

She also showed me how she made a Swiss fruit tart. She lined a tin with sweet pastry, then put in the elderberries mixed with orange peel which she had saved and crystallized in a jam jar with sugar. She then poured over a sweetened egg custard and baked it in her Baby Belling oven.

I was delighted at such ingenuity, and thus began my love of Continental fruit tarts.

Built in 1953, St Peter's third vicarage adjoins the church on the northern side

BELSIZE Remembered

# Painter Ben Nicholson

*Adam Sonin*

A short man, immaculately dressed in an informal style of his own devising, often sporting a flat cap and wide collared shirt with various layers, Ben Nicholson (1894-1982) certainly looked the part of an artist. He was born at Eight Bells, in Denham, Buckinghamshire, on April 10, the eldest of four children of painter Sir William Newzam Prior Nicholson (1872-1949) and his first wife, Mabel Scott Lauder Pryde (1871-1918), also a painter.

Ben Nicholson (left) with fellow artist Victor Pasmore in 1960
*Photo: Felicitas Vogler, courtesy British Council Archives*

The family were not affluent but moved in good society, and Nicholson's father was known to be a man of style. Family friends included the writers Rudyard Kipling and Arnold Bennett and the artist Walter Sickert, with whom they spent summer holidays in Dieppe. Sir William Nicholson painted a portrait of the 44-year-old creator of Peter Pan, J M Barrie, who invited him to design costumes and sets for the stage version. Nicholson junior recalled:

"After a lot of art-talk from our visitors my mother said that it made her want to go downstairs and scrub the kitchen table… I always remember my mother's attitude when I came to carve my reliefs."

The family moved houses many times in Hampstead, Bloomsbury, Chiswick, Woodstock and Rottingdean. In a letter Nicholson described the interior of one of the family homes. "Terrific elegance in my parents' home – Chippendale chairs & Dighton prints, & white panelled walls & an enormous chandelier and Aubusson carpets."

Alongside this refinement there were a lot of interesting domestic objects. The letter continued to describe the domestic setting: "For as long as I can remember my home was full of the most lovely spotted mugs & striped jugs & glass objects which [my father] had collected." Nicholson inherited his father's passion for collecting and one of his early works, dated c.1911, is in fact of a striped jug.

Between 1904 and 1906 the family lived at No.1 Pilgrim's Lane, in Hampstead. Years later, as an adult, Ben Nicholson was to return to the area to live and work, first during the 1930s when he occupied the Mall Studios, off Tasker Road, in Belsize Park and later in the '70s and '80s when he returned to live on his childhood street, this time at No.2 Pilgrim's Lane.

He attended the Slade School of Fine Art, in London, from 1910 to 1911, and cemented a friendship with fellow pupil Paul Nash. In 1912 Nicholson spent a year learning French in Tours, France and decided to become a painter rather than a poet. During his stay he received a letter from his painter father suggesting "Why not do both? Blake did."

As an asthmatic, Nicholson was deemed unfit for military service in the First World War, and from 1917 to 1918 he travelled to the United States to undergo an operation on his tonsils and later travelled around the country.

On November 4, 1920, Nicholson married Winifred

Roberts, also a painter. The couple had three children and formed a working partnership which was mutually beneficial. Nicholson later recalled that he learned a great deal about colour from Winifred and a great deal about form from his second wife, Barbara Hepworth.

Ben Nicholson and wife Barbara Hepworth
*Photo: Humphrey Spender*

In 1931 Nicholson met the sculptor (Jocelyn) Barbara Hepworth (1903-1975) at an exhibition in which he was exhibiting alongside her first husband, Jack Skeaping. During that summer, the pair met again while on holiday with, among other notables, Henry Moore and his wife Irina, and fell in love.

Nicholson and Hepworth started to share a studio in Hampstead in 1932 and at this time Winifred moved to Paris. In order for Nicholson to see his children he, and Hepworth, would pay regular visits to the city. On one such occasion they dropped into Picasso's, who showed them "a miraculous succession of large canvases... from which emanated a blaze of energy in form and colour".

Back in Hampstead the couple shared their experiences with Henry Moore and other artists in their community. On November 17, 1938, the couple were married at the Hampstead Register Office following Nicholson's divorce from Winifred earlier that year. Nicholson and Hepworth had triplets in 1934, two girls and a boy.

In 1938 the artist Ben Nicholson was instrumental in bringing his friend, the Dutch artist Piet Mondrian, to Belsize Park and to safety from the Nazis. His hospitality was further extended by lending the émigré a bed for his new rooms at 60 Parkhill Road, in Belsize Park.

The artist once swapped his still-life oil *Jug and Playing Cards* for a white alabaster carving called *Head* made by another friend, Henry Moore. Moore treasured the piece all his life. The writer Herbert Read called the area in which they worked in Belsize Park "a nest of gentle artists".

Art historian Dr Sophie Bowness, Hepworth's granddaughter and a trustee of the Hepworth Estate, said: "He [Nicholson] shared with his father, William, a love of puns and practical jokes. He was a determined avoider of formality and convention and disliked personal publicity. His singleness of purpose and dedication to his work were absolute.

"Nicholson was critical of intellectual approaches to art that lacked intuitive feeling and poetry. He was a very perceptive writer on art and a marvellous letter-writer."

A blue plaque was erected by English Heritage in 2002 at 2B Pilgrim's Lane, Hampstead, Nicholson's home from spring 1974 until his death in 1984.

**Adam Sonin**
*Ham&High*, April 2013

1940-43 (two forms) by Ben Nicholson, oil on canvas
© *Angela Verren Taunt. All rights reserved*, DACS 2012

Belsize Park Gardens, near England's Lane, c.1900

Belsize Park Gardens, 2012

ARTISTS OF ALL KINDS

# Painter Lancelot Ribeiro
## *Marsha Ribeiro*

My father, the painter Lancelot Ribeiro (1933-2010), first came to Britain in 1950 as a teenager. He had left Bombay that year to arrive in a "grim, bomb-damaged city, subject to rationing that had been in force since 1940".

His older brother, the artist F N Souza, who had arrived a year earlier, met him at Tilbury and took Lancelot to lodge with him and his wife, where their lives "were an 'open book' intertwined at Chalcot Square".

Lancelot Ribeiro had been sent by his mother to Britain to study accountancy. Success was to prove elusive. Soon abandoning accountancy, Ribeiro went to study life drawing at St Martin's School of Art before he was conscripted into the Royal Air Force in 1954.

Eight years later, after a spell back in Bombay, where he had established a name as a successful painter, my father decided to settle permanently in the UK. His young wife (my mother) followed him with her 15-month-old baby. Their early lodgings were in various cramped London addresses, but they soon gravitated towards Belsize, where my father established a home and studio.

*No.41 Belsize Park Gardens*

*Lancelot Robeiro, photo provided by M Ribeiro*

Their first real home occupied a spacious first floor at No.41 Belsize Park Gardens, which looked out onto expansive tree-lined streets and provided an oasis of calm. His brother was by then a stone's throw away in Belsize Square, where a circle of their literary and artist friends would often gather.

It was in this studio that Ribeiro painted his oils: towering townscapes, basilicas, steeples and spiky trees. His experiments with polyvinyl acetate and oil mixes marked the start of faceless and often monstrous heads, one of which was later to hang above my bed. Before long, his trademark style had crept onto a sliver of wall, my hand-crafted 'early learning' toys and our furniture. While I was growing up, his studio offered an Aladdin's Cave of delights to explore. Hugely colourful worlds hung from our walls, while pots of powdered colours of every hue, jars of PVA, and relics of wood constructions provided ample distraction for me. >

Haverstock Hill in the sixties, my mother recalled, had a J. Sainsbury butchers and, two doors down, a Sainsbury bakery, an Odeon cinema (now Budgens) and the "Chocolate Box" sweetshop [p166]. Hardly any traffic. Up in Hampstead there were galleries which have since disappeared, including the Mount, New End and the Everyman Foyer Galleries in which Dad's work appeared.

Belsize Park tube station still had manually-operated hand-cranked lifts, with iron folding gates which took passengers down to platform level where impressive burgundy trains, with wooden floors and lush upholstered seats, would draw in. Hazy tobacco smoke-filled carriages were the norm in those days. Return fares 'into town' cost the equivalent of 40 pence and were dispensed by the wonderfully Victorian aqua-blue ticket machines. Push-button panels in each carriage and suspended ball hand rails just beckoned to be played with.

At Whitestone pond, donkey rides were still available to children and, on occasion, could be found at the main entrance to Hampstead Heath. In 1980, my father moved into an attic flat in No.214 Haverstock Hill. His kitchen looked out onto the striking red-brick Hampstead Town Hall and I would often wave to him on my way back from the Rosary primary school. At the back, we could see the tennis courts and, beyond that, the nature reserve where my class would be taken for our eagerly-awaited afternoon 'Nature' studies, before work on building the Aspern Grove estate had started.

As I grew older, Sundays were occupied with cake-baking or slow roasting a chicken interspersed with long afternoon walks on the Heath and Parliament Hill. We often took a cooked lunch to sit under our favourite cluster of trees. This inspired a short but intense watercolour phase in Ribeiro's work; a series of naturalistic scenes of tree landscapes and wild grass scenes before he again went abstract. I vividly recall our path through South End Green, taking in a small art shop, Rumbolds bakery and the Classic cinema, now an M&S simply food.

A sizeable post office served the area where we opened our first savings accounts. It was soon replaced by a short-lived florist and then Costa coffee. Chez Nous was the first café to appear on Haverstock Hill, soon followed by a Copenhagen patisserie (now a GBK burger chain), replacing a long-standing Italian restaurant that had seemed, to us, over-priced and unwelcoming. The Screen on the Hill cinema (now the Everyman), sporting a flying duck emblem, added an element of excitement to us as kids in the Rosary and then a Café Flo which has had a restaurant in its place ever since.

In 1987, my mother and I moved into Holmefield Court [p62] on Belsize Grove. The block had several émigré residents from the Second World War who regularly held animated gatherings in the garden before the yuppie generation started to take over. We had heard from them that the Art Deco block had had a fairly regal past with a resident liveried porter, and a swimming pool, now built over. An Indian restaurant, eventually converted to flats, faced the garden. At No.40 Belsize Grove stood the Garrett Anderson Maternity Home (one of three choices given to my Mum when she was expecting me).

Facing the intriguing deep-level wartime shelter stood a Midland Bank, a florist/grocers ablaze with colour, a novel 'Le Provençal' delicatessen and a well-established off-licence. The kosher Grodzinski bakery was a particular favourite. Further up, the Dewhurst butchers, then a newsagents and later a 'Maxwell of Ealing' fish and chips shop were to appear and then disappear.

I have always felt deeply rooted to Belsize. Even when my work took me away from London, it continued to exert a certain pull on me. It is one of a few places that have retained their character and long attracted artists and writers alike. Coming 'home' I felt at peace like nowhere else I could imagine and a sense of heritage that continues to run through my veins.

From 'Retracing Ribeiro' a project sponsored by the Heritage Lottery Fund

ARTISTS OF ALL KINDS

Lancelot Robeiro, *Landscape,* c.1965, oil on board

Lancelot Robeiro exhibition, Burgh House & Hampstead Museum, 2016

BELSIZE Remembered

# Painter Peter Hedegaard
## *Isolde Hedegaard*

Peter Hedegaard and I, Isolde, moved into a studio house in Glenilla Road in May 1963. Peter, originally from Copenhagen, was a painter and had regular exhibitions here and elsewhere. I did his screen printing in the studio.

Peter Hedegaard's studio, *photo provided by I Hedegaard*

The house was always lively and chaotic, with children and friends. Our two children and their friends played in the house and the garden, and also in the street where they made friends with others living across and along the road.

When we arrived in Belsize Park it was a very different place. There was a butcher, a baker and a large old-fashioned cinema on Haverstock Hill, an Express Dairy, another butcher and a do-it-yourself shop in the Village. Crescent Fruiterers is the only one of the original shops left. Peter hunted around in vain for a café where he could have a coffee mid morning and read his paper. In the early 1970s, however, the area began to change. The large old Odeon cinema was turned into Budgens and the Screen on the Hill cinema. The traditional post office together with butchers, bakers and most of the old-fashioned useful shops disappeared, and soon there was no shortage of cafés. In the Village we had the Late Late store where one could buy a pint of milk at 11pm, something unheard of before then. Fundamentally, however, it has remained an intimate place with the feel of a village where people still bump into others they know on the way to the newsagent or a café.

We had come to Belsize Park quite by chance in the first place because Peter happened to find a studio house suitable for his work and our family life. It turned out to be an extraordinary place in which to live, particularly for an artist, surrounded by a large number of other artists who became friends, exchanged ideas, socialized, saw each others' work and exhibitions and sometimes also shared them.

In 1970 an exhibition was held at Swiss Cottage Library of Camden artists who lived and/or worked in Belsize Park and who were all producing abstract painting with a focus on colour. The exhibition was called Colour Extensions. Apart from Peter Hedegaard it included Michael Kidner, Edwina Leapman, Peter Kalkhof and others.

They were a tiny minority of all the artists living in Belsize Park whom Peter knew and with whom we shared the vibrant artistic and intellectual life of the 60s and 70s in this small lively patch of London.

Peter died in 2008, survived by two children and four grandchildren. His estate is represented by Rocket Gallery [Sheep Lane, Hackney] where his work has been shown in two exhibitions since his death.

ARTISTS OF ALL KINDS

Peter and Isolde Hedegaard
*photo provided by I Hedegaard*

The children (on bicycles) with friends in Glenilla Road
*photo provided by I Hedegaard*

Rocket Gallery, 2013
*Photo: © Paul Tucker, courtesy Rocket Gallery*

BELSIZE Remembered

# Painter Robert Bevan
## Three Paintings of Belsize Park

Robert Bevan (1865-1925) was a painter, lithographer and draughtsman. Bevan was perhaps the first English painter to use pure colour in the 20th Century. From 1900 he lived at No.14 Adamson Road, Belsize Park.

The painting below is a view from the artist's house in Adamson Road. Robert Bevan's studio had originally belonged to painter Sir Alfred East [p8]. Bevan's style was well suited to express the solid, rectilinear character of the domestic architecture in this area of London. He fully exploited sunlit effects in his streetscapes and relished describing the crisp tonal relief pattern of regular, interlocking geometrical forms in terms of cleanly differentiated planes of colour, each sharply defined in outline.

The original Metropolitan Underground Station, now demolished, stood on the corner of Belsize Road. Bevan knew how to profit from the lessons of the Impressionists, the Fauves and the Pointillists. He went to Pont-Aven, and was also influenced by Gauguin. The effects of these contacts are apparent in his mature work. Robert Bevan's London street scenes, which include those painted in Belsize Park, were rather more favourably regarded than his landscapes.

*Swiss Cottage*, Robert Bevan, 1912

The third painting is a scene at the junction of Belsize Park and Buckland Crescent. The large house in the centre is No.69 Belsize Park and was originally known as the Belsize School (founded in 1889), later to become The Hall School. The artist's son, R A Bevan, was a pupil there until 1913 when he went on to Westminster School. The Junior School started in 1917 and the building was used for The Hall Junior School from that date.

*Houses in Sunlight*, Robert Bevan, 1915

*A Street Scene in Belsize Park*, Robert Bevan, 1917, *Museum of London*

Buckland Crescent from just beyond The Hall Junior School

BELSIZE Remembered

# The Birth of Pentameters Theatre
## Léonie Scott-Matthews

I moved into Belsize Park in September 1961, to No.3 Glenloch Road, a large, light room – the nicest I'd seen – in a semi-detached house at £2 10/- per week. In my final year at the Royal Academy of Music and Drama, studying for the RAM Diploma and LRAM (Speech and Drama), I found Belsize Park to be the ideal area – a quiet road, but with handy shops, restaurants, pubs and transport on my doorstep.

In the mornings I would walk to Finchley Road and catch the bus to Baker Street, then walk along Marylebone Road to the Royal Academy. On Fridays, I remember passing popular pubs like *The George* on Haverstock Hill and *The Roebuck* on Pond Street on my way to what is now the Overground station at South End Green, to catch the train to Dalston Junction where I did teaching practice at Gayhurst Primary School. I would often gather leaves, grasses and flowers from Hampstead Heath for nature studies.

Belsize Park proved to be very sociable and friendly, and I got on well with the other occupants of the house. Our favourite restaurant was the Witch's Cauldron in Belsize Village. My friend Jennifer was cashier there and when she needed a night off I would take over from 8pm for payment of 10/- and a lovely supper. The atmosphere was great, a room in the basement with checked tablecloths, candlelight, carafes of red wine and young waitresses. I can still taste the food today – avocado vinaigrette, chicken chasseur and a chocolate dessert.

On leaving the Academy, I moved to a smaller, cheaper room in the same house and started my career as an actress. First job was ASM at the New Chelmsford Civic Theatre. The director Charles Vance had hired a Hollywood star, Guy Rolfe, for the leading role in the opening play *The Marriage-Go-Round*, and each morning he would drive up to collect me from my little Belsize bedsit in his Rolls-Royce. As we drove to the theatre he recounted hilarious tales of his latest film – *Taras Bulba* with Yul Brynner and Tony Curtis.

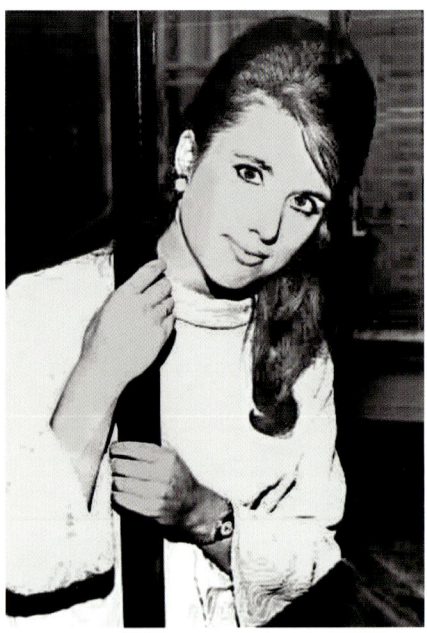

*Léonie Scott-Matthews in 1968*
Photo: Nigel Sutton, Ham&High, Sept 1968

After that came *Toad of Toad Hall* at the West End Comedy Theatre, with local actor and director Michael Blakemore playing Badger. For this I would take the No.24 bus – later made famous by Adrian Mitchell who wrote a musical play about the bus when he lived nearby.

During this time I also worked with a friend Robert Sheaf and his organisation, the Playgoers Club, arranging theatre visits in conjunction with editing a magazine. We enjoyed walking around my area discussing and arranging theatre events, writing poetry and plays and visiting the local cinema, restaurants and pubs.

I had the idea of living and working in the same area, doing something I was really passionate about, and this thought started slowly to take root.

This is how Pentameters came into being: a poetry, music and theatre venue which opened on 7 August 1968 at the *Freemasons Arms* on Downshire Hill. By this time I had moved from Belsize to Hampstead Hill Gardens. During the summer of 1970 Pentameters used an open space at Parkhill Road (back to Belsize!), kindly lent to me by the owner. There we erected a mobile stage and put on poetry, music and theatre, including a Tennessee Williams play.

The next move was to the *Haverstock Arms* from 1970 to 1971. We had an enormously successful year there with poets, musicians and actors. Particularly memorable evenings were with poets Roger McGough, Adrian Henri, Brian Patten, Dannie Abse, Adrian Mitchell, William Burrough's colleague Sinclair Beiles, South African poet Denis Brutus, American poets Louis Simpson and Marilyn Hacker, Sir John Waller, Sidney Carter and Robert Calvert (collaborator with the rock group Hawkwind).

I first met Harold Pinter (who was later to act in his play *The Dumb Waiter* at Pentameters) in the bar at the *Haverstock Arms*, where he had come to see his friend Henry Woolf perform. Not recognising him I asked him what he did, to which he replied, "I sort of write!"

The *Pentameters Anthology of Poetry, Art and Essays* was published by Magpie Press with cover by Mal Dean and original work by poets such as John Heath Stubbs, George Macbeth, Paul Ableman, Sir William Empson, Kevin Crossley-Holland, Libby Houston and Keith Johnson of Theatre Machine.

Finally, we were able to take up residence above *The Three Horseshoes* (which subsequently became *The Horseshoe*) at No.28 Heath Street in Hampstead.

Thank you, Belsize Park, for starting me on my journey. The Pentameters Theatre celebrates its 50th anniversary on 7 August 2018.

*The Horseshoe* Heath Street, 2017

BELSIZE Remembered

# Pianist Alice Herz-Sommer

## How Alice's music blocked out the evil of the Holocaust

Alice Herz-Sommer, who died aged 110, was known as the world's oldest Holocaust survivor. A celebrated concert pianist, in 1943 Alice was taken to the Theresienstadt internment camp in what is now the Czech Republic with her son, Raphael.

Alice Herz-Sommer, photographed by her grandson on her 109th Birthday
*Photo: Ariel Sommer*

Her skill as a pianist helped her survive, as she was forced by the Nazi guards to give concerts. It was, she said, an extraordinary thought that music could be powerful enough to go some way to block out the extreme evil she saw around her.

Born in 1903 in Prague, Alice was one of five siblings. Her father, Friedrich, owned a factory that made weights and scales. She began playing the piano aged six and by her teens was playing professionally. She once recounted the story of how her sister was being courted by a man named Franz. He would appear on Sundays and ask permission to take her sister for walks. Her father would allow this if Alice accompanied as a chaperone. She remembered the handsome young man telling wonderful stories as they walked. His surname, she noted, was Kafka.

In 1931, Alice married Leopold Sommer, a violinist, but their life together was cut short by the Nazis. Leopold died of typhus in the Nazi death camp of Dachau, in March, 1945. Alice would later be given a tin spoon from a friend who took it from Leopold before he died: she cherished the memento of her husband for the rest of her life.

After the war, Alice emigrated to Israel and lived there until 1986, when she moved to London, aged 83, to be closer to her family. She settled in Belsize Grove, and neighbours recall the sound of her daily piano practice wafting through the corridors of the flats she lived in.

Alice has been the subject of books and documentaries. Her autobiography, *A Garden of Eden in Hell*, published in 2006, was translated into seven languages (the US edition is titled *Alice's Piano*). Her story was featured in the film *We Want The Light* and, more recently, *The Lady in Number 6: Music Saved My Life*, which has been nominated in the 'best documentary' category in this year's Oscars [2014].

Royalties raised from her book established a scholarship named after her son to study at the Guildhall School of Music. It was, say her family, a source of great contentment that her life had generated enough interest for people to want to hear about it – and provide funds for music students.

A favourite pastime for Alice was enrolling in lecture courses organised by the University of the Third Age, based at Hampstead Town Hall. Visiting lecturers would often end up at her house, fascinated by her story and inspired by her enthusiasm for their subjects.

Alice had simple tastes. For breakfast, she would eat a slice of bread spread with Greek-style yogurt or honey, while her family recall her sometimes "boiling everything else she ate till it was dead 1,000 times over". She loved chicken soup with carrots, potatoes and onions, and only drank hot water with lemon. She never drank alcohol, and found pleasure in other people's company – and, of course, her music. She would go swimming at Swiss Cottage, practise the piano for up to five hours and then have friends over.

Alice held firm views on different composers: she loved Bach because she said he represented "pure logic", and his music could be considered in terms of the mathematics of tone and rhythm. She also loved Beethoven and Chopin, and enjoyed most other forms of classical music. She was not, however, keen on opera, though she made exceptions for Mozart, as she felt it was comedy and the music was wonderful. She also admired jazz, for the virtuoso talents that it attracted.

Alice is survived by her two grandsons, David and Ariel.

**Dan Carrier**
*Camden New Journal*, February 2014

Belsize Grove c.1870, *archive*

BELSIZE Remembered

# Writer Eva Tucker

## Born Berlin, 18 April 1929. Died Hampstead, 12 November 2015

Friends and visitors to Eva Tucker's large book-crammed living room in Belsize Park Gardens – she moved into the flat with her philosopher husband, John, in 1966 – would have the wonderful impression they were in at least two worlds. There was the warm feeling of German-Jewish hospitality, with Kaffee und Kuchen liberally supplied, and there was the sense of a writer's lair, with scattered manuscripts, magazines and books, and the writer herself bright-eyed and curious for news and ideas.

A widow since 1987, with her long skirts and tied-back hair Eva might have been presiding over a literary soirée from the time of her two literary heroines, Virginia Woolf and Dorothy Richardson. Not that she was in the least old-fashioned in mind or opinion; she simply took little interest in passing fashion or style while being open to whatever was going on in the arts she so passionately loved.

Eva was born Eva Steinicke. Her father, Otto, was a communist journalist, and her mother, Margot, was Jewish, the daughter of Felix Opfer, a much-respected doctor who lived with his wife on the fashionable Friedrichstrasse.

For Eva, her grandparents' comfortable flat with its grand piano, pictures, and books, was a kind of paradise. But not for long. As things got nasty in Germany, her father, who had contacts with English Quakers, arranged in early 1939 for his wife and daughter to escape by boat to England where Margot worked as a maid and then in a munitions factory, while Eva was sent to a Quaker school in Weston-super-Mare. These experiences became the source for Eva's much-praised novels: *Berlin Mosaic*, published in 2005, and *Becoming English* in 2009. (Both books were gathered into one, *Belonging*, in 2014 and published by Starhaven Press.)

Back in Germany, things did not go well for Otto who was killed by a bomb in Berlin, or for the Opfers – he died in Theresienstadt and she in Auschwitz.

Eva never forgot these tragedies or her tempestuous relationship with her pleasure-loving mother, safe in England, and they became the subject of a very powerful 1997 Radio 4 documentary, *When She Comes Back*, which was made in collaboration with her daughters Judith, Catherine, and Sarah. In fact they haunted much of her other work, including short stories and plays for BBC Radio.

Eva's wide reading and bilingual gifts led to other work for radio, notably adaptations of Joseph Roth's *The Radetzky March* and Robert Musil's *The Man Without Qualities*, as well as pioneering work on the then neglected novelist Dorothy Richardson. All of this, together with critical writing, lecturing, and mentoring younger writers, led to her becoming a Fellow of the Royal Society of Literature in 2009, an honour of which she was immensely proud, as she was of her three daughters, taking great pleasure in Judith's successful artistic career, Catherine becoming a Church of England priest in Southwark's most culturally diverse parish, and Sarah's work as a group analyst and psychotherapist.

There was one other setting for that Belsize Park living room: between the 1970s and the 1990s, the coffee and cakes were laid on the big wooden table for a circle of "seekers after truth": Quakers (Eva was one of them), Anglicans, Baptists, Buddhists, Congregationalists, Hindus, Jains, Jews, Methodists, Muslims, Presbyterians, Roman Catholics, Unitarians, and a subtle sprinkling of Atheists. Eva, as chair and host, was in her element.

**Piers Plowright**
*Camden New Journal*, November 2015

ARTISTS OF ALL KINDS

Belsize Park Gardens from the south side in 2012

Preserved ironwork
Belsize Park Gardens

BELSIZE Remembered

# A Bedsit in Uryland

*Jean Clarke*

Some of the best years of my life were spent at No.14 Glenmore Road, where I lived in a bedsitter for 11 years from January 1961 to February 1972.

The house was one of several in the area owned by Peter Ury, who along with his mother-in-law, whose name I can't remember, seemed to have property in every street. They both owned large houses in Daleham Gardens where they lived on the ground floor, letting all other rooms out. I named the five houses he owned in Glenmore Road (numbers 10 to 18) Uryland.

Each house had about nine tenants, living in various sized bedsits, each of which had a small gas ring for cooking, hand basin and gas fire. Everybody had their own meter for electricity and gas. There was one toilet and one bathroom which had a meter into which you put a shilling which gave enough hot water to bath in.

I was lucky enough to live at the back of the house on the ground floor, in what was originally the kitchen and scullery of the house. This meant that I had a room of about 10ft. square with a small kitchen off. I also had a garden which I shared with the chap in the next room as I did the outside loo. It was fantastic to have our own toilet which I cleaned diligently and used throughout the year – even digging through the snow in the winter. The house loo was a hit and miss affair with all tenants having to supply their own loo paper. How glad I was to be out of that!

We were a motley assortment of people from various countries. My first neighbours were Austrian sisters, one a nurse, the other a seamstress. They were followed by an English chap who stayed almost as long as I did. We had a lot of battles over the garden but on the whole got along very well. I remember an American girl who regularly shop-lifted in Bond Street and another who was a hostess in a night club. Her Japanese boyfriend eventually moved in with her. They have been married for 30 years and still live in North London.

Uryland had a good community feeling. Everybody was very friendly and when rooms became free we usually co-opted a friend into the house. The general feeling was that although we had not the luxury of flat sharing, we had no petty fights over domestic chores or payment of bills. I was lucky enough to have a gas cooker in my kitchen and enjoyed cooking. This resulted in my usually cooking Sunday lunch for anybody who was around. We each contributed about a shilling, I bought a joint and veg and everybody came to my room with a plate and knife and fork to eat. I had few chairs so we sat on floor, bed or wherever there was a space. It was not unusual for 10 people to be there.

We had lots of parties which went on all night but I have no recollection of complaints from neighbours. Maybe because most of them were there! The parties usually went on till about 6am, by which time we were exhausted. Visitors slept on the floor and everyone else crept back to their room. My garden was put to good use. I cut the grass regularly with shears, but fortunately there was not much – just enough to picnic on and have scrabble tournaments.

A launderette arrived in Belsize Village although I think most of us did our washing by hand at home. I was very generous with my washing line, allowing anyone to dry their clothes in the garden. There was a small delicatessen run by a very nice Asian man next to the tube station. He very kindly cashed cheques for us when we ran out of money at weekends. This was before debit cards and cash points, and many of us were dependent on him.

I decided to keep a housekeeping log book. Everything was recorded, and I still have the book which I kept for a year. It is fascinating to compare the cost of living in 1961 with today.

A friend and I took a nostalgic walk around the area about two years ago. Gone are the bedsits, now replaced by expensive flats. We spoke to a friendly lady who was tending her garden who asked why we were looking with such interest at the houses. We told her that we had lived in the road in the 1960s when it was full of bedsits. She then invited us in to see her house which was so beautifully restored that it was hard to work out exactly where our rooms would have been.

I am still in touch with several of the Uryland crowd, which proves how strong our relationships were in those days.

Two pages from Jean Clarke's 1961 log book

Glenmore Road, c.1905

BELSIZE Remembered

Taking a quiet nap – at least as far back as the late 1970s, generations of ginger cats have lived at the top of Glenloch Road

Before the Glenloch Investment Company developed this part of Belsize the area in the 1860s was known as the Eastern Coppice
*archive*

# Bohemian Belsize Park
## Alan Mickelburgh

I have lived in Glenloch Road for over 40 years. I always drew pictures and did a lot of painting. I never exhibited my art work though everyone tells me I should. I have also somewhere a play or two I wrote and some poems. It was a very bohemian area, full of bedsits in those days, 1960-70. But what we had then has disappeared now. Every fortnight the windows were cleaned all down the street. There used to be a man going around calling out for sharpening knives. Fishmongers, fish and chips shops, proper butchers. The man who used to run the butchers took over the fish and chips shop.

The *Belsize Tavern*, Belsize Village, *archive*

I used to drink at the *Belsize Tavern* and the Monty Python crowd used to drink there as well, except for Michael Palin who went to another pub. Twiggy came there with her then husband. She regularly threw glasses and drinks at him in the pub.

Another character was an eccentric American woman who kept rabbits in her house which used to run around everywhere. She told us they were toilet trained. Rabbits used to gnaw at her telephone wires regularly. We had summer parties out in the garden. One summer the American woman with her long legs jumped over the fence to join the party. That was the first time we met her. Another character called Oswoldo Citri lived on the same street, an Italian, he always had some wild stories to tell whenever I met him.

I used to write a lot of letters to the papers, mainly about Hampstead Heath and people trying to stop fishing in the ponds. There was a woman who used to call me a barbarian every time she walked past me.

Once our landlords – a couple of Polish chaps – took the roof off as a ploy to get us out. Water poured into the flats. But I didn't want to budge. Eventually they went to jail for what they did. It was the time when Rackman and other landlords were trying to get people like me out of our flats.

I remember an occasion when hailstones came down lasting for about two hours. It was a real deluge and people's garages got blocked and they couldn't get their cars out.

I was an opera lover and so went into town to Covent Garden and the Albert Hall. It's easy to get into town from Belsize Park. I had good friends like the cartoonist who did the front page of the *Telegraph*, Tony Holland, he lived in the Village, Ronald Frazer a TV personality, the actor James Villiers – all good friends I drank with at the *Belsize Tavern*. There was someone else called Elephant Bill. He had lived in Africa at some time or other and acquired that name. When I was stuck in hospital Tony Holland drew a wonderful cartoon card for me that I still have. He was a good companion and a good spirit.

BELSIZE Remembered

# From Bedsits to Baby Buggies

*Alison Hawkes*

Someone should do a demographic survey of Belsize Park, and compare it with the profile when I first moved in here, some 44 years ago.

Of course, there are a lot of physical changes. Many of the buildings were run down and multi-occupied then, and it was definitely considered a poor relative of already affluent Hampstead. Most houses were sub-divided into relatively small flats, some 320 of which were owned by the Church Commission and others by the Eton College estate. The shops on Haverstock Hill included two old-fashioned J. Sainsbury shops, no Budgens, and the Odeon cinema was dilapidated. It was very unlike today's bustling scene, with flourishing cafés and restaurants spilling across the pavements.

Many of the residents were involved in the arts. In my road alone, I was assured by one of their number, there were 18 artists and many others involved in writing or journalism. So it was the clack of typewriters or the slap of paint on canvas that you were likely to hear if you walked down the street. Most of these people were relatively poor, and more than a little bohemian, with stew and cheap red wine served for Saturday night gatherings.

The first house I lived in briefly during the mid sixties was occupied by many, and you never quite knew who was staying there. There was a diffident figure in a mac who slipped in and out now and then – apparently, he slept in the old billiards room! When I asked who he was, I was told "his name is Woody Allen – some sort of American comedian". Later, the British Surrealist manifesto used to be hammered out on a manual typewriter by the genial artist Conroy Maddox, who lived in the flat above mine.

Apologies if my nostalgia is showing a bit. But when I compare then with now, there is another even more crucial difference – the number of children. I'm not saying there weren't any children being raised in Belsize Park in the old days, of course there were, but there were definitely fewer of them. Most of my neighbours were childless or empty nesters. When a family moved into the road, it was an event.

Today, you can't go anywhere in Belsize Park without being aware of children and their conveyances. Baby buggies, each vying with the other in size and splendour, jostle each other and you on the pavements and in the shops. 4x4 vehicles convey older children to school or to leisure activities. Playgrounds and libraries and cafés are crowded with kids and their parents. And you're more likely to hear a baby crying or the sound of children at play than a painter or writer at work.

This transformation of a suburb has largely come about as the houses that were cut up into small flats have been converted back into family homes. Belsize Park, once a despised adjunct of Hampstead, has become desirable in its own right, to the astonishment of the old guard. I first realised this when a godson stayed with me about 15 years ago. When he told his workmates where he was staying, they were immensely impressed. Pop stars and film actors lived there, he was told.

Of course, we've all benefited from the rise in property values along with the rise of Belsize Park, and the influx of families has brought new life to the area. But am I the only one who still hankers a little for the days when bohemianism and fun were Belsize's chief characteristics?

BEDSIT LIVING, FRUGAL BUT FUN

Alfresco dining on the wide pavements of Haverstock Hill

BELSIZE Remembered

# From Colombo to a Home in Belsize
## *Ranee Barr*

It was only after some months I realised how lucky I was to come to live in Belsize Park. The year was 1973. I had arrived here straight from Colombo, Sri Lanka. I found the area to be so very lush and green compared to other parts of London, with Primrose Hill and the Heath within easy walking distance.

Belsize in those days was filled mostly with one-room living called 'bedsits'. I had such a bedsit and shared the bathroom on the landing with others in the house; the rooms were small, fitted with a Belling cooker and a sink in the corner. It was hard getting used to that style of living.

I first had a room in Adamson Road, then for a short time in Belsize Park Gardens (a room with no window but a square of glass set into the roof) and then at No.34 Primrose Gardens, where I regularly missed the house when walking past because they all looked the same! Much later I would be fortunate enough to be able to purchase a place in a mansion block in Belsize Grove.

Apart from buying a piece of fruit or two from the greengrocers opposite the tube station, I usually made my way to the Belsize Village shop that sold pasties. Often this would be dinner while I watched my clothes as they washed at the launderette. It's strangely comforting to see the launderette is still there today. There were other shops in the area that I never went to, like the dark interior of a delicatessen on Haverstock Hill with rows of hanging sausages, and the small chocolate shop [p166] wedged in a corner of Belsize Grove.

There were restaurants, if one could afford to go to them, like Chateaubriand in the Village. Also the Hill House Restaurant (opposite the Old Town Hall) with an ancient fire engine parked on the forecourt. But I regularly went to the coffee shop that served amazing apple strudel which was part of the Cosmo restaurant in Finchley Road.

I spent most of my Saturdays at the lovely little library in Antrim Grove. Apart from reading it was a place to stay

The Hill House Restaurant, Haverstock Hill, *archive*

warm on cold winter days. Bedsits were never warm enough, invariably due to a draughty window or inadequate heating.

Cucina in England's Lane was a favourite for browsing as was the bohemian market in Swiss Cottage; goods were displayed on the ground or on trestle tables under the London Plane trees. It was a pleasant way of spending a few hours on a Saturday as there was almost always someone strumming on a guitar.

One Christmas Eve I made my way to St Stephen's Church and was surprised to see there was hardly anyone there for the service, also the building had a musty smell about it. Now I know the church was built with a flow of underground water running down to a river nearby. This probably contributed to the damp. Not long after the church closed its doors a squatter moved in and sometimes you would see him in the front garden clearing up and lighting a small bonfire. I believe he was allowed to stay there as a sort of guardian of the place; he remained there for many years until the building was about to be restored.

In the early days a few elegantly-dressed ladies could be

seen on Haverstock Hill in their long fur coats; I was told they were the German-Jewish refugees who'd come here to escape the war. But by the time I bought a flat in Holmefield Court there was only a sprinkling of these ladies living there. They were all very strong characters with an accent to match!

The bedsits were disappearing in the 1980s when developers got their hands on houses to convert them into flats. Families and couples were moving in.

The face of Belsize was changing. New cafés were opening up: Tootsies on Haverstock Hill and Camomile in England's Lane. And Chez Nous café on Haverstock Hill – to this day retaining its original decor.

Stanley Gardens c.1908, *archive* renamed Primrose Gardens

Primrose Gardens near the junction with England's Lane in 2012

BELSIZE Remembered

# Furnishing from Skips
## *Helen Pollock*

My partner would see to the furnishing of the house by 'skipping'. Haverstock Hill is in an affluent part of north London and the kind of thing he retrieved included colourful vintage clothes, costume jewellery, an African ebony carved Nubian head, ivory chess pieces with a marble board, three ladder-backed chairs and a superb tall ecclesiastical candle stand in wrought iron. He furnished the flat and clothed ourselves and our kids in the years when we struggled, never being flush.

The skip recycling felt like a rescue mission. My partner would go for his regular exercise late at night, avoiding the frenetic activity of the day. At that hour he didn't have to worry about traffic and excitable pedestrians and could go at his own speed, when the streets were quiet and everyone asleep except for foxes, late revellers, the odd dog walker, housebreakers and those after the lead from roof tops, the occasional police car and other skip hunters. The saddest but most rewarding skips were outside the houses of elderly people who had died. The houses were being rapidly emptied by relatives keen to sell the house and oblivious of the lifetime's accumulated treasure of the deceased.

We had a friend who owned a flat in Amsterdam and she told us that there is a particular day each week when households put out their unwanted furniture. Anyone who passes simply picks up what they want, and at the end of the day a council removal van collects the surplus.

Discarded items in a skip in Belsize Park

BEDSIT LIVING, FRUGAL BUT FUN

Haverstock Hill, 1934, *archive*

Haverstock Hill, 2010

37

BELSIZE Remembered

# Happy-Go-Lucky Days
## *Beverley Rice*

Having previously lived in Cannon Place which was very quiet I was surprised to find how different the atmosphere was in Belsize Park, vibrant and friendly. In the early 1970s I shared a basement flat in Steele's Road with four other twenty-somethings. At this time the street had not been gentrified and was an ideal venue for our not infrequent parties and constant trickle of friends passing through. Our parties were always popular. There was a cleaning rota but alas this was not always adhered to. Most of our beds were propped up on large party-size beer cans but at least we had a constant supply. What chaotic and enjoyable times we had. One drawback was that your breakfast might disappear during the night, not eaten by mice but by someone's boyfriend who happened to get the munchies at 3.00am.

Steele's Road, c1900, *archive*

We frequented the *Sir Richard Steele* pub and also *The Washington* on England's Lane, but the *Belsize Tavern* in Belsize Lane was probably our favourite haunt. In those days the pub had sawdust on the floor to soak up the spills. The pub also had its own off licence.

Belsize Village and the surrounding streets were full of bedsits and multi-occupied flats. It was a very cosmopolitan area. People a long way from home made an effort to be sociable. A popular stop-off was Conrad's Bistro opposite the pub (previously known as The Witch's Cauldron). Further down Belsize Lane was a café the Greasy Spoon (not its real name which I cannot remember). Nowadays it has been unrecognisably transformed into Oliver's Village Café.

I wonder how many people remember the old man who ran the ancient clock-mending shop in the Village. He was as old as the shop or was it that the shop was as old as him? There was also Fur Clean where a larger-than-life character called Mike worked, collecting and delivering all manner of furs. Next to the pub was Sybarites, a hairdressing salon run by a very amiable chap called Russell. Inside the shop he had an interesting collection of artefacts salvaged from salons of bygone days. There was a character called Alan, known as Alan The Hat for obvious reasons. Alan never went anywhere without his sketch book or hat. I wonder whatever happened to the numerous sketches he made of people and places. There was also Canadian Gordon who played the flute and when The Abraxus opened on Belsize Park Gardens – we didn't go there to work-out, we went to listen to Gordon sing, play the guitar and flute.

The area attracted arty and theatrical types. I remember a group of young men who wore identical dark suits and went everywhere together, it was like a living theatre. The actress Rita Tushingham lived in Belsize Lane and Twiggy lived in Belsize Crescent and would pop into the little supermarket for the odd pint of milk. Once or twice I spotted the actor Jonathan Pryce in the vicinity of *The Washington*, also a TV Weatherman, I think his name was Francis.

Happy memories of the Belsize Festivals, which brought people old and young together. Rides for children and everyone spilling out of the pub to listen and dance to the live bands situated on the very small triangle in the middle of the roads. No pedestrian area then. People who had moved far away would make the annual pilgrimage for the festival, catching up with old friends and to gossip about life in the village.

For a while I lived in a house on Belsize Lane with three other girls and about this time met my future husband in the Village. We married in Hampstead Town Hall on Haverstock Hill which was next door but one to the hotel – not sure if it was The Post House in those days. I remember sitting in the hotel with my future sister-in-law waiting until it was time to go and sign my single days away. We moved to Adamson Road for a short time and then moved to Belsize Park to an attic flat in one of the huge houses.

We liked being near the Village and this was fine until our baby came along. With 76 stairs to struggle up with baby, buggy and shopping it was not ideal. Being so high up we had a good view over rooftops. In the early hours of one morning (possibly 1978) I was sitting up feeding the baby and noticed lots of smoke in the distance which eventually became quite thick and then lit up the skyline quite spectacularly. Next day I discovered the School Hall at University College School on Frognal had burnt down.

Eventually we moved to NW8 to a flat minus the 76 stairs. I missed the buzz of the Village and maybe that is one of the reasons that many years later I was lured back to the area by a job in Belsize Lane, but of course things never stay the same and the soul of the Village went when the *Belsize Tavern* closed and sadly the Belsize Village Festivals are no more.

Belsize Village, 1905, *archive*

BELSIZE Remembered

# Wartime and After

*Robert Labi*

Before the war there was the big influx of refugees, especially from Austria and Germany. My mother came from Vienna in 1938 and for a time she used to wait in Swiss Cottage to see if she recognised anyone from Vienna. And she did: she found two childhood friends who had also escaped from Vienna.

When I was young it was still possible to communicate in German with the older assistants/owners in some local shops if you wanted to. After the war there was a brief far-right/fascist campaign to force the refugees to leave the area. Even in the early 1960s some roads, like Belsize Grove, still had significant numbers of residents with Germanic family names. Rents were comparatively cheap, which made it possible for the refugees, who had in many cases lost everything they possessed, to live in Belsize Park.

There still are a number of physical reminders of the Second World War in the area, notably the entrance, at the corner of Haverstock Hill and Downside Crescent, to the deep shelter. There are also shelter entrances at the Belsize Avenue side of the old Town Hall.

Underneath the small triangular piece of green at the end of Eton Avenue opposite the Central School of Speech and Drama [p165] there was an Air Raid Wardens shelter. I know about this because my mother, then living in Adamson Road, was a Warden and told me about it. Early in 2013 the metal door to it had become exposed as the grass covering had come off.

A number of houses had air raid shelters built. There was one at the rear of No.12 Belsize Park Gardens (where I lived between 1951 and 1958) and it was only in 1998 that my parents knocked down the shelter in the back of their garden at 79 Belsize Park Gardens.

Of course for children in the 1950s the bomb sites and blast-damaged areas were our adventure playgrounds; I remember one in Fellows Road and the large area, adjacent to St Paul's primary school which then was located in Winchester Road, where the Hampstead Theatre is now, 100 Avenue Road and the Swiss Cottage Centre (although some houses were demolished to make way for this centre). By the late 1960s the Swiss Cottage bomb site partly became a large, free, council-maintained car park, almost encircling the local British Legion club at the Finchley Road end of Eton Avenue.

Haverstock Hill was, until the 1960s widening of Finchley Road and the redevelopment of its south side into Harben Parade, an important everyday shopping area that had, amongst other shops, two old-style, counter service Sainsbury shops (one selling fruit, veg and dairy products and the other meat), a Mac Fisheries store, butchers, bakers and other such shops. The Sainsbury stores closed when the company opened a supermarket on the Finchley Road. Similar changes took place, on a smaller scale, in Belsize Village and England's Lane.

The steady lifting of war-time rent controls from the late 1950s changed the area, as people (including those who had been housed in the area after being bombed out as well as the refugees) had to leave. Belsize Park began to be posh.

BEDSIT LIVING, FRUGAL BUT FUN

The entrance to the deep level shelter in Downside Crescent
– used today as a data storage facility

Belsize Park Gardens at the junction with Glenilla Road, 2011

Gabrielle Coudron and Marion Ford Anderson outside No. 41 Belsize Park, the Ford Anderson home, c.1914
The Andersons were cousins by marriage to Nobel Prize winning author John Galsworthy and it has been said he based the *Forsyte Saga* on them
*Photo provided by John Hibbert john@hibbertfamily.org*

COMMUNITY

Belsize resident Nigel Kennedy and Friends performing for locals in St Peter's Church, 2013

Belsize Village Delicatessen in 2011

43

BELSIZE Remembered

# A Bit of Bengal in Belsize

## Debi Bose Harvey

Belsize Park is the place my father, Bidhan Bose, called home for 18 years after he left India. It's where my mother, a new bride in her 30s, set up her household. It's where my sister and I were born. It's where the Kolkata Bengali diaspora celebrates Ma Durga. For us, Belsize Park is more than just a place to live in Zone 2.

My father moved to Belsize in May 1957. His one-bed flat soon became a place where other students and young couples from Kolkata came to socialise, eat food that reminded them of home and share stories. We call that adda.

He occupied various flats in and around the area, finally settling into No.26 Belsize Park with his wife, Meera Bose in January 1969.

The small flat was in a house occupied by other Bengali families and couples. My mother recalls how it was akin to living with your best friends, popping into each other's homes for a cup of tea and a gossip. The bonds and friendships created then are still strong today.

Belsize has been the place to be seen for Bengalis each October since 1961. At Durga Puja time, which is held at Hampstead Town Hall, Bengali families in their finery would stroll down from their homes on Belsize Park to celebrate for five days with like-minded Bengalis from all over London.

Since those days of the 1960s and early 70s, Belsize Park has been synonymous with Durga Puja outside of Kolkata. The party afterwards was held for many years at the Post House Hotel, as it was known then, and subsequently at *The George* across the road.

The second-generation Bengalis have maintained this tradition and have introduced their spouses (who may be from other cultures) to the tradition too. It is still a sight to see today, several generations in their finest saris, sitting in *The George* after Durga Puja has finished, all linked by a family tie to the Belsize Park of the 1960s.

Even though many of us have moved away, Belsize Park still represents a home from home for Bengalis, a place where the strong supportive community is still very evident today, as the photograph opposite shows.

My father is very ill now, but despite his dementia, his memory of Belsize Park is very much intact.

On the steps of No.26 Belsize Park, *photo provided by D Harvey*

COMMUNITY

Paired villas just beyond No.26 Belsize Park viewed from the garden of St Peter's Church

Durga Puja at Hampstead Town Hall in 2012, *photo: Sagar Barua*

BELSIZE Remembered

# Belsize French Club
## *Marion Hill*

It was while I was manager of Belsize Library that Marion Bieber, who had given a talk about life-long learning and the U3A to Belsize PLUG (Public Library Users Group), suggested we consider setting up a club for European Languages. This would fulfil a dream of hers – to give people the opportunity to hear and speak different languages and learn about the accompanying cultures – and also help the library by giving it some 'out of hours' use and bringing new people in.

We held a meeting in June 2002. Those who met were keen, but too few in number to form a viable club. We decided we would nevertheless organise a French evening in October and see how that went. In the meantime I was moved to a different position in another library but, by arrangement with successive managers and the cooperation and indeed active support of the Belsize Library staff, I was able to continue as the library contact and key-holder for what became the French Club @ Belsize Library.

For the first four years, the Club was run by 'the two Marions'. In the summer of 2006 Marion Bieber, who had already lived with cancer for a year, announced that she would not be able to continue running the club. Ronwen Emerson agreed to take over the bulk of the administration while I continued as the library and publicity contact.

Marion Bieber nevertheless prepared and ran the October 2006 meeting and came to the February 2007 Valentine's Day evening to lead the conversation for those not wishing to play Scrabble. At the April meeting we heard that Marion had just gone into the Marie Curie Hospice. Unfortunately Marion died in April that year. It so happened that our next meeting was a talk about Marie Curie. From money collected that day and cheques subsequently sent in we were able to make a donation of £100 to the Marie Curie Hospice in Marion's name. In October 2007 we celebrated our 5th Birthday conscious that the best tribute we could give Marion was to ensure the French Club continued to thrive and develop.

When I retired in May 2010, we were able to continue meeting at the library for another year, with the chair of the Friends of Belsize Library as key-holder. With mounting costs and uncertainty over the library's future, we moved to the Hampstead Town Hall for a year – and changed our name to the Belsize French Club.

We were grateful for the welcome we got there, but always hoped we'd be able to return to the library. We took part in meetings about the library's future and anxiously awaited news of developments. Although we usually have a summer break we accepted the Winch's invitation to hold a meeting in August 2012. And then, in October 2012, we were able to celebrate our 10th Birthday back 'home' in the Belsize Community Library. We reminisced over French wine and apple tart and Librarian Cina led us in song, and then continued with our monthly meetings.

The aim of the French Club is to enable people to practise and develop their language skills through a variety of activities – play readings, discussions, talks, playing Scrabble. We've had a varied programme thanks to the number of members and visitors able to give a talk or lead a discussion. We've also invited people to talk about their holidays, their favourite poems, books, films, paintings and recipes. There's no teaching as such but we've been fortunate in having French-born people attend so we are able to help one another out. Belsize Library has been an ideal venue and serving some refreshments at the end of each meeting has helped to create a friendly atmosphere and to enable members to get to know each other.

COMMUNITY

Belsize Library, c.2010

The original Belsize Library in Antrim Road, c.1900, *archive*

47

BELSIZE Remembered

# The Beginnings of Belsize's PLUG

*Susanna Duncan*

At the end of 1987 Camden Council was in financial straits and decided to close the Shaw Theatre, St Pancras Reference Library and several branch libraries, including Belsize Library. There was a great deal of public protest. Petitions were sent, the matter was reported in *The Times* and finally the Camden Public Library Users Group (PLUG) was formed, based at Chalk Farm. Staff at St Pancras and other libraries went on strike. There was a sit-in by a group of men who spent four days and nights in the Reference Library to prevent removal of the books. The actor who was starring in *Winnie-the-Pooh* in the West End paid Belsize a visit before Christmas.

Our campaign took place from January to March 1988. The threatened closure date was March 14. At a public meeting here in January 1988 people were asked to write to the Mayor of Camden, the director of libraries (Christine Wares) and others who influenced library closure decisions and to the press.

Roy Charterton, vice chair of Camden PLUG, called on volunteers to form a committee. A number of people came forward and the adhoc defence committee held weekly meetings in members' homes. When I first joined in February they met at Evelyn Bacharach's house across the road. This is my diary entry for that day: "Fifteen people. Very active and intelligent. Nice pastries." I immediately became minute secretary. I remember a message from Catherine Lambert, dynamic chair for several years – "Thank you so much for the invitation. As I am now 90 and tire rather easily, I am afraid I will only be with you in spirit at the party. I shall raise my evening glass of sherry and drink a toast to the Friends of Belsize Library."

To return to the campaign. We attended meetings of Camden Council and I especially remember Flick Rea, Aileen Hammond and Huntry Spence speaking up for the libraries; a Lib Dem, a Labour and a Conservative, two of them members of PLUG. We pushed circulars through people's letter boxes and put up posters all over the place. Some were designed by the artist Dorothy Ralphs, primary school children made some quite touching ones which we put up in the library. The council told us to remove them so we stuck them on the fence next door.

Many people wrote to the press. The *Ham&High* and the *Camden New Journal* were very supportive in publishing articles and covering our events. There were meetings in the old Town Hall chaired by Melvyn Bragg, who urged the audience to organise action. Throughout the campaign and to this day we have had the support of prominent writers including Margaret Drabble, Beryl Bainbridge, Jonathan Miller, Alan Bennett, Katherine Whitehorn and Diana Athill.

We arranged a poetry reading by actors Simon Ward, Frances Tomelty and poet John Rety with an audience of 90. I quote from the Belsize Residents Association's Newsletter – "this moving, well-attended event drove home the point that enriching the mind is what open libraries are all about".

An opinion poll was conducted on the library steps one Saturday to see if people would pay 50p a month to keep the library open. The overwhelming majority said they would.

Early in March we had a Spring Fair organised by Evelyn Bacharach. There were stalls around the library with goods provided by the local community. This is my diary entry: "I manned a table with china ornaments, pale pink cats and high heeled shoes in blue, yellow and pink ceramic (porcelain), very hot tomato soup and baked potatoes supplied by Elaine Hallgarten. I bought four dinner plates, one of which is still in one piece. We packed up at teatime and I helped Evelyn count the money. We had taken nearly £1,000 for our fighting fund".

On March 7, one week before the projected closure date, the All Labour Council Group heard a deputation from the

Belsize Library and decided to recommend saving it. The next night a Policy and Resources Committee did the same for the sake of the elderly living nearby. A crew came to the library to make a film for the *Getting On* TV programme about the effect of library closures on the elderly. The emphasis at the time was on old people, but it seems that nowadays there are more young people in the library, and especially children.

At the next meeting of our defence committee we formed ourselves into the Belsize Public Library Users Group, the first individual PLUG in Camden, and planned to support the library with lectures, exhibitions and other activities. This was soon put into practice and has never ceased. I think we were the first PLUG to have these talks. We have a long tradition of excellent speakers, both famous and less well known; the prose and poetry readings initiated by Catherine Lambert were particularly successful and I believe unique to this library.

Closure was again threatened in 1992. Catherine Lambert wrote "We held an overnight sit-in after one of our poetry readings, jolly uncomfortable and cold! But local television came and we had press coverage". And PLUG, with Catherine as Chair, went to the High Court.

There have been subsequent threats, but resistance to the council's policies is widespread and is continuing.

Belsize Branch Library late 1930s, *RIBA archive*

BELSIZE Remembered

# WWII and Hillfield Court

## *Melanie Price*

Like so many Londoners, I was neither born nor raised in London as I am a Devonshire lass, but I moved to the big city permanently in 1984 and since that date my home was initially in Belsize until we moved to the adjacent South End Green. I had already spent a couple of years in London when I first started working in 1970, and shared a flat with some girls in a house just behind Waitrose on Finchley Road (John Barnes department store in those days), so I gravitated to north-west London right from the start.

I moved to Brussels in 1972 and lived there for nearly 12 years, and during this time I met and married my husband, a fellow Brit, and our son was born in 1983. But we always knew we would be returning to the UK one day, so we bought a flat in Hillfield Court on Belsize Avenue in 1981 as an investment, and rented it to a charming Japanese family for the first couple of years.

We returned to London and moved into our flat at Hillfield Court in the spring of 1984. We enjoyed living in our lovely two-bedroom corner flat for over two years before moving to a house near South End Green, where we continue to live today.

I have very happy memories of life in this comfortable, solid mansion block which backs onto the Old Town Hall. It has the unique advantage of a lovely enclosed garden for the private use of the occupants – a rare gem in this crowded part of the world!

Hillfield Court was built in 1934 on land that had originally formed part of the Belsize Estate. Just six years later this mansion block took on a small – but vital – role in the defence of London.

During the Second World War, barrage balloons were going up over cities, airfields and other key sites and by the middle of 1940 there were nearly 1,000 over London. Hillfield Court played host to one of these balloons, which

Typical WWII barrage balloon

was anchored to a large concrete block set into the lawn. Incidentally, the block is still there, but the only evidence is an unevenness in the current manicured lawn.

The barrage balloon was tethered to the block with a number of metal cables to defend against low-level aircraft attack, damaging any aircraft on collision with the cables, thereby making flying in the vicinity extremely treacherous.

A few members of the RAF Balloon Command were billeted in one of the ground floor flats of Hillfield Court so they could be ready to launch the balloon when necessary. I also understand that a brick bunkhouse was built in the grounds of Hillfield Court for the RAF team, and this is currently used as a very sturdy garden shed!

Hillfield Court, Belsize Avenue

Hillfield Court Lawn, 2012

BELSIZE Remembered

# Life in Holmefield Court
## Stephany Feher

I have lived in Belsize Grove for over 60 years. First at Gilling Court, and then in Holmefield Court.

I was born in Berlin in 1921. My life in London started in an unexpected way during the war. I was in Prague with my family when Hitler entered the city in 1939. On the same day my parents put me on a train to London. I had no money, no English, nothing. When I arrived in London I lived for a short time in Golders Green as an au pair.

I moved to Belsize Park not long after. It was very different from the way it is now. There weren't many cafés then, but we had a furrier, a big chemist next to the tube station, a good Continental delicatessen on the same side, a German bakery, and the post office.

There was a small restaurant between Gilling Court and Holmefield Court to serve the two blocks. Lots of us ate there. The cooking was mainly Continental.

Holmefield Court in those days was a fun place to be. I was never bored. There was a community feeling with lots of people my own age to talk to; we sat by the pool, or went up onto the roof where there were tables and chairs. We spent most of our time up there sunbathing and partying. They were marvellous times.

We also had two porters to the block, dressed in a smart red uniform with gold buttons down the front and gold epaulettes.

The big swimming pool at the back had to be covered up during the bombing because of the reflection of water, an easy target for the bombers. In time it became a flowerbed and continues to this day to be a beautiful garden. You can still see the outline of the pool.

After meeting and marrying my husband, who was Hungarian, we first lived in a studio flat in Gilling Court. After seven years of marriage I became pregnant and went to the landlord and asked to be moved to a bigger flat. We were then moved to Holmefield Court, where I still live, in the same flat. But in between this time we went to live in Newcastle-upon-Tyne until the war was over. Then we returned to Belsize Park and never looked back.

During the bombing I never went to the shelter in Belsize Park Underground station. "Not me" I said, "I am staying here". I remained in my flat with blackout curtains, but my husband who was afraid of the bombs went to take shelter in the Underground along with scores of other people packed in like sardines.

Havercourt next door was bombed and was badly damaged. My mother-in-law moved out of there to go and live in Watford the very day the bomb fell. She had a lucky escape.

I have loved and still love the area. Hampstead Heath over the years became my favourite place to visit every weekend. I have bought many paintings from the open air art exhibitions by Whitestone Pond.

Now everyone in Belsize Park knows me. In Holmefield Court I had so many friends in the early days, but now I make new friends all the time when I go every day to Chez Nous for my morning coffee at 9.00 a.m. and then return again at 12.30 for my lunch.

There is a tremendous sense of community feeling among the cafés and shops along the parade. I can't think of anywhere else where I would have wanted to live. Belsize Park is a marvellous place.

Stephany Feher outside Holmefield Court in the late 1960s
*photo provided by S Feher*

COMMUNITY

Holmefield Court, 2016

BELSIZE Remembered

# Better than Hampstead
## *Deborah Buzan*

Our rented, purpose-built flat near Crouch End wasn't much to write home about and was an overlong bus ride from town, at least for this young married couple. So in the mid 1970s we bought our first home: a roomy and bright two-bedroom flat on the lower end of Frognal. We could just about say we lived in Hampstead – not that we were snobs, mind you – but when it was time to upsize, we knew we'd have to move downmarket – to Belsize Park, for instance. Belsize was becoming fashionable in the late 70s, with gentrification making inroads into the bohemian bedsit-land of the previous decades. There were lots of handsome buildings, and Primrose Hill was nearby. The neighbourhood had character, too, which Hampstead, despite its elegance and classy reputation with my family back in America, seemed to lack.

The flat in Lambolle Road had lots of rooms and a big garden – well, expanse of weeds – but was un-modernised, had no central heating, and one of the rooms even had a dirt floor with the old boiler in it from when the house was a single dwelling.

The renovation took so long we had to move in with the builders: us with our cat in one room and most of our worldly possessions in another. Once it was completed, I soon felt at home and not just because there was an artist living on each side of us.

Almost all of our neighbours lived in converted houses, some of them in very small flats indeed. One nearby house was divided into 19 bedsits until a couple bought the whole building and somehow managed to re-house every tenant. They, like us, were part of a flood of upwardly-mobile incomers.

Over time, other 'neighbours' included the London Go Centre, a Rajneesh Centre, several sports clubs and a College of Fine Arts (all of which occupied a site nor far from us). We liked the Rajneesh Centre with its calm aura and orange-clad members. It had a sign in the bar that read "Champagne is also vegetarian", and its cafeteria served inventive meals. That in itself was impressive, given the quality of most restaurant food in the 1980s. Of the pubs in the area, we tended to frequent 'the Wash' on England's Lane.

When I was editing the Belsize Residents Association's Newsletter a decade or so ago, I commissioned a piece by another neighbour, Stephen Barlay, about being a newcomer to the area. His charming article began: "My wife, Agi, and I moved to Belsize Park just about a year ago. We now know it was a great mistake. We should have done it thirty years earlier." Indeed. In 1979, when we moved here, this was a part of London that didn't initially whisper 'come hither', but which was actually a really fine part of London in which to live.

There were elements of a real neighbourhood society also then. On Guy Fawkes night, for example, some hundreds of people would gather on the crown of Primrose Hill, where the local community association built a huge bonfire, and set off a superb fireworks display from the level ground at the foot of the hill.

Those were magical occasions, with the fire embers making a warm glowing circle three yards in diameter. But eventually the event got too big, and in 1998 it was briefly taken over by Camden Council and then quietly shut down, probably on health and safety grounds.

COMMUNITY

Street party in Lambolle Road to celebrate the wedding
of Prince William and Catherine Middleton in 2011

Distinctive houses on Lambolle Road, south side, 2011

PRIMROSE HILL COMMUNITY ASSOCIATION
FIREWORK DISPLAY AT 7·30

8TH. NOVEMBER
ON PRIMROSE HILL

GUY COMPETITION AT 7·15
SOUPS, BAKED POTATOES, HOT DOGS, CHESTNUTS
& COKES AVAILABLE

BELSIZE Remembered

# The Belsize Festival

*Judith Nasatyr*

Starting in the mid-1970s the Belsize Festivals were organized by local groups. What was noticeably different to present-day local events was the fact that the organizers were comparatively young people (some are still active in Belsize Park).

Camden gave a grant for local festivals and we held fund-raising jumble sales to supplement the grant. We got together with creative (and authorized) squatters in Winchester Road to make masks for a stall and some youngsters made a midnight trip to London's garment industry area to collect bags of discarded luxurious fabrics that were used to make bunting. There were games stalls, apple bobbing and plate smashing. At intervals throughout the day musicians including a steel band entertained the crowds. There was a fire eater and Morris dancers too.

I remember the first festival best. It had been a miserable summer but that September weekend was warm and sunny. The atmosphere was wonderful, people were taken by surprise, residents who had not been involved in local events before or since joined in and helped.

Belsize Festival poster from 1974

Belsize Festival, 1975
*Photo: Henry Grant*

BELSIZE Remembered

# The Cosmo Restaurant
## Remembered as 'saviour' for Jews fleeing fascism

A plaque commemorating a café once considered a 'sanctuary' for Jewish refugees fleeing Nazi oppression was unveiled by the Association of Jewish Refugees (AJR) in November 2013 at its former home in Finchley Road.

The Cosmo, also known as "Sigmund Freud's favourite caff", was legendary among north London's Jewish community and found itself becoming a home away from home for those forced to flee violence spreading through central and eastern Europe.

Originally opening as a coffee bar in 1937, its servings of goulash, Wiener schnitzel and apple strudel provided refugees – many of whom came from Vienna and Berlin – with familiar tastes and smells.

Ursula Trafford, 86, and husband John, 94, both refugees who celebrated their wedding at The Cosmo in 1957, returned along with dozens of former customers to reminisce about their former 'safe-haven'.

"We used to sit in this dining room for hours – it was just such a warm and friendly atmosphere," said Mrs Trafford.

"We would obviously talk about what was going on in our homelands and in the war, but mostly we were just eager to meet other people like us.

"This country saved us and The Cosmo became the kind of sanctuary we needed to help build a new life in London."

As Belsize Park and Swiss Cottage became the new home to more and more refugees, The Cosmo's dining rooms – which now form part of an Indian restaurant – came alive with countless dialects.

Behind every conversation in Hungarian, German, Russian, or Yiddish, one would find a story of the persecuted who were fleeing far-right regimes and anti-Semitic barbarism.

Marion Manheimer, 63, whose parents took over The Cosmo from its former Hungarian owners in 1957, said its role as a 'sanctuary' was symbolic for her family.

"My father left Berlin to escape the Nazis but lost many members of his family," she said. "He would hire people he met on his travels and the place became full of people who had come to north London to escape fascism. It was also a great place for a conversation."

When talk strayed from how the streets of north London compared to former homes in mainland Europe, psychoanalysis was often a common talking point.

The café was a favourite haunt of Sigmund Freud, who lived a stone's throw away in Maresfield Gardens, and the proximity of the Tavistock Centre in Belsize Lane meant the restaurant's 1950s panelled dining room remained full of 'psychobabble'.

But while the décor and conversation remained unchanged, the outside world moved on. Slowing business and rising rents meant the restaurant was forced to close in 1998. The AJR hopes the blue plaque will preserve the memory of the building's former role.

Frank Harding, trustee of the Association of Jewish Refugees, said: "The Cosmo for many years was able to recreate an ambience similar to the one its customers came from."

**Paul Wright**
*Ham&High*, November 2013

[The AJR plaque disappeared in 2014 and in 2015 the premises became an ice cream parlour.]

COMMUNITY

Marion Manheimer, whose parents ran The Cosmo
with John & Ursula Trafford and Frank Harding
*Photo: Nigel Sutton*

The Cosmo interior, *archive*

BELSIZE Remembered

Window of a house on Eton Avenue

Cycling down Eton Avenue

COMMUNITY

# The Great Storm

## *Helen Pollock*

The wind was getting up one October night in 1987 when my partner started on his usual late-night bike ride about 3 am. He noticed that nobody was in the street and how quiet it was everywhere, with broken branches and dustbin lids lying on top of drifts of fallen leaves.

Then he heard it. A rustling like rain in the distance, but there was no rain. His hair began to lift and he thought "I'll be blown off my bicycle". Flying down Eton Avenue, avoiding trees that had crashed to the ground, roots in the air and a maelstrom of debris, he could feel no wind but a kind of heat, with warm air around him. He felt he was at the very eye of the storm.

The phenomenon was extraordinary and he was somehow singled out to be king of the hurricane. He could have joined the sailing frenzy of estate agent boards, some still attached to their two-by-four posts. He felt exhilarated, with an excitement that he had never known and he did not want the feeling to stop. He jumped off the bike and the rubber band holding his hair together broke loose so that his long red hair whipped his face sharply. Tears from the wind and the flying road grit stung his eyes. The magic had reverted to more normal ordinary expectations.

London, in fact, had experienced its first blackout since the Blitz, in what Douglas Hurd, the Home Secretary, described as "the most widespread night of devastation in the South-East since 1945".

*The Times* front page following the Great Storm on the night of 15-16 October 1987

BELSIZE Remembered

# Sarah Gould's Diary of Good Works
## January 1885 - December 1890

Sarah Gould lived at No.3 Steele's Road in Belsize Park. Born in 1841, she died in 1926, aged 85. Sarah was 44 when she wrote this diary, described as a 'Six year record of an uneventful life'.

Sarah Gould's Diary

No.3 Steele's Road was the home of Miss Sarah (Sai), and her older sister Miss Louisa (Lou) Gould. The house was rented from 1885 for a period of seven years. Although they could be considered well off, they still needed a loan of £50 from the family solicitor to be able to move there from Woburn Square.

Also living in the house was Miss Yates, or 'Y', an invalid lady aged 70, who had been housekeeper to their father and a companion to the sisters. The sisters had to stay at home in order to look after their invalid father, John Gould FRS, who was an ornithologist, bird artist, and publisher of a number of monographs on birds. He died in 1881. Their mother, Elizabeth Gould, had died in childbirth when Sai was born in 1841.

After Lou died in 1894 Sai bought a house on Rosslyn Hill.

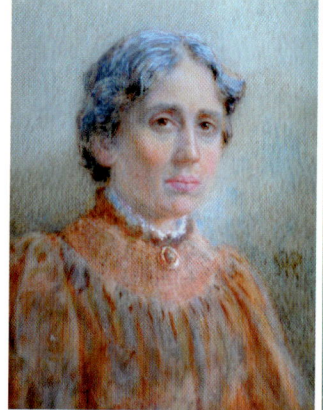

Sarah Gould and Louisa Gould by Henry Robertson

**Highlights from the Diary**
**Servants:**
There was a cook and two live-in housemaids, named Agnes and Emmie. Agnes stayed for nearly four years. Sang at concert at Unitarian Mission. Emmie and Agnes sang hymns with Sai on Sunday evenings. In 1886 arguments in the kitchen. After she left Sai found the new maid had better manners, Agnes had got 'too uppish and familiar'. She married but Sai wrote that 'her husband has bad health, the marriage can hardly be a prosperous one'.

**'At Home' Events:**
Lou's new musical instrument was a Harmony Flute. 'It makes a charming accompaniment to the piano. Our neighbours next door thought it was a violin.' The sisters also bought a 'Magic Lantern' for children's parties, and a billiard table for adults. They were 'At Home' on Wednesdays for visitors.

**Bus Conductors:**
**Sa**i became friendly with a Mr Shaw, who helped her on the omnibus. "Caught omnibus at the 'Adelaide'. Conductor's hours were from 9-11 and 40 minutes for dinner, same for tea. Half-hour some other time of the day – 2 or 3 days a month holiday. 'Hampstead men much better off than some

No.35 Steele's Road

Louisa on the Heath

of the lines.'"

Sai visited his [Mr Shaw's] family often. New baby, born 15 September 1885 called after her Isabel Sarah Elizabeth, christened in St Luke's Kentish Town, 'short coated' at 6 months in a pretty red petticoat. Bobby, her brother, came to her children's parties.

Through the Unitarian Mission, Sai met Mr Weatherly, a conductor and cab driver who was often out of work. Baby 'thin and delicate'. Sai arranged for two boys to have a fortnight's holiday in Harrow. She sent money for coal, and provided Christmas dinner. His cab licence ran out and Sai gave him some money. 'Broker' arrived for overdue rent, Sai paid £1.2s.6d but Mr Pollard said she was wrong to pay rent to families as some had low morals.

**Lending Library:**
Sai collected storybooks from friends and opened a library in her house in August 1885 to August 1889. Sent circulars to Rhyl Street. For poor neighbours and children with a reference. Mrs Shaw unable to borrow because she could not read.

**Doctor:**
In 1890 Dr Alford came almost every day to see 'Y'. £24 fee for six months.

**County Council:**
Voted 1888 for a member of the Municipal Council for London. 'It is quite a new experience for us to vote.'

**Neighbour:**
Mr Henry (Harry) R. Robertson was a close friend. Exhibited oils for Royal Academy exhibits, miniatures and etchings. Had a studio in Steele's Road. Painted 'Magic Lantern' slides for the children's parties. Painted miniatures of Sai and Lou in 1894.

**Unitarian Mission:**
Rev J. Pollard took Sai to see poor families in Rhyl Street, e.g. a tailor with one room and family of 5, eldest girl in rags. She was given an 'area' and visited the sick and new babies almost every week.

Mrs Brown had buried six babies but 'thanked the Lord they were in Heaven'. She and five of her children came to a Jubilee Party at Sai's home. Sai went to the Free Christian Church on Sundays.

**Entry for Monday January 2nd 1887:**
'A snowplough with eight horses went down Haverstock Hill.'

Thanks to the diary owner Dr Anthony Edelsten and to Maureen Lambourne who provided David Percy with these extracts from the diary and grateful thanks to Caroline Warner of Steele's Road

## Agatha Christie: the Mystery of the Lawn Road Novels
*Gene Adams*

Everybody has read Agatha Christie's comment about the ultra-modern 1933 Bauhaus-style Isokon flats being like a "giant liner" without any funnels, and most know that she was one of several famous people who once lived there, but that is often as far as it goes.

Inspired by the wonderful exhibition held at the British Museum ('Agatha Christie and Archaeology', November 2001-March 2002), I thought it would be a good idea to add a bit of background to the quote – after all I live opposite the flats which we now call Isokon after the firm of the original owner Jack Pritchard.

Agatha Christie, *archive*

The Lawn Road Flats (Isokon building) c.1934, *archive*
Now one of the historically significant buildings in the UK

Agatha Christie lived in the Lawn Road Flats, as they were then called, at No.22, from 1940 until 1946. Her husband, the distinguished archaeologist Max Mallowan, was working for the Air Ministry in Cairo. Their friend Professor Stephen Glanville, also an archaeologist, was already living in the Lawn Road Flats and helped Agatha to secure hers. It was wartime and Agatha, on her own, was in London throughout, suffering all the fears and privations of the bombing.

Agatha was doing voluntary war work as a hospital dispenser, in which she was well trained from voluntary work which she, as a young woman, had done in World War I. During World War II, while living in Lawn Road, her daily routine was at the University College Hospital, from which she sometimes walked home when the tube trains were not running properly, and her evenings were spent writing.

She was at the height of her powers and fame as an author, and her war-time years at Lawn Road were extremely productive. Not only did she write several of the well-crafted crime novels we all know, but she was also very involved in writing for the stage, which she loved – and novels under the pseudonym of Mary Westmacott.

In addition she wrote a charming and entertaining memoir of her recent happy years accompanying her husband on archaeological digs in the Middle East during the 1930s, *Come, Tell Me How You Live*. This was written as a 'homecoming present' for her husband Max, who returned to England in 1945. It is not only very informative about her love of archaeology but also reveals a delightful humorous, witty personality and obviously a very likeable character.

Day-to-day life during the war in London was insecure and frightening. Whole buildings and streets would disappear overnight and no one knew whether they would survive to see the next day. Some friends of Agatha "harboured a small cache of tinned ham and olive oil for her, in case Lawn Road was knocked flat". Thus fortified, wrapped in Max's farewell present of a warm Jaeger dressing gown, she worked away on her noisy, state-of-the-art new typewriter, in her smart modern flat, both her own works and long letters to Max.

Stephen Glanville, their good friend, helped Agatha in her thriller writing, a vital source of income for all of them, by providing her with scholarly information about ancient Egypt. The result was *Death Comes as the End*, unusually set in ancient Egypt, and later, a play called *Moon on the Nile*.

In return for Stephen's professional scholarship she provided him with a sympathetic ear, listening to his complicated and apparently disastrous love life. But when it became too much for her she would take refuge in her flat and in her own words, "lie back in that funny chair here which looks so peculiar and is really very comfortable".

By 1945 when the war ended, life in London must have been extremely dispiriting and uncomfortable. Agatha, anxiously awaiting the return of Max, but uncertain of the precise date of his arrival, decided to take a weekend in Wales to "get away from the flat". After a long tiring journey she staggered back to the flat in Lawn Road on Sunday evening, carrying her suitcase and a couple of kippers for dinner.

"I got weary and cold," she wrote later, "and started turning on the gas, throwing off my coat and putting my suitcase down. I put the kippers in the frying pan. Then I heard the most peculiar clanking noise. I went out on the balcony and looked down the stairs. Up them came a figure burdened with everything imaginable, clanking things hung all over him. This was Max. He might have left yesterday. He was back again. A terrible smell of frying kippers came to our noses and we rushed into the flat. What a wonderful evening it was! We ate burnt kippers and were happy."

They stayed in the flat until 1946, so Agatha had spent the better part of six years there, mainly on her own, while her husband was abroad. When they at last were able to reclaim their requisitioned (by the Navy) house in Devon in 1946, things began slowly to return to normal and they finally departed.

Marcel Breuer, Long Chair, 1935-1937, *Courtesy of Burgh House and Hampstead Museum,* considered to be the pinnacle of achievement in furniture design in the 1930s. Gene Adams, (then voluntary Curator at Hampstead Museum) acquired this rare example of an original in plywood by the Isokon Company donated by the architect Nicholas Wood in 1996.

Isokon building, 2013

BELSIZE Remembered

# At Home in Parkhill Road
## Wendy Richards

Here I'm trying to entice passers-by to sit and join me awhile and try my homemade elderflower cordial, elderflower pancakes and homemade cakes. This is all in aid of collecting for our local hospice, whilst the parking wasteland of concrete turns briefly into a colourful garden with raised flower beds.

Wendy collecting for the local hospice, *photo provided by W Richards*

Strangers stop at the gate and linger to introduce themselves as neighbours we never knew we had, and often stay on for a game of scrabble and conversation. Our maximum is twenty people and we make sure we have spare seating so folk can circulate. This, to me, is like the old days of gatherings in our homes for lectures, discussions and music, often when trios performed on their balconies. Often too there was the exquisite aroma of fruit cakes baking for the guests.

The elderflower season reminds me that I would take the home-made 'champagne' to revive the bell ringers after a long session at St Martin's Gospel Oak. I realised they needed refreshment, even more if they'd failed to complete the changes. Everyone knew the culprit, who had spoilt the round by not watching, not counting meticulously, but no name was ever mentioned.

My love affair with bicycles began when I paid 21 guineas (a thief's bargain in 1950) with my first ever wages. This all-steel Raleigh locked in the fork and carried me many miles until it was stolen. I had no accidents except once when cycling along on a slippery road, I slid off along with the gingerbread men I'd just baked for 40 primary school pupils. After difficult days of teaching it was a joy to freewheel down the hills homewards. This sturdy bike carried me safely from London to Brighton on charity rides. The roads were cleared of traffic and we aimed to speed along towards the sea and arrive before the pubs shut. There was also the reward of sea bathing and visiting friends in Hove. It seemed we were going downhill all the way until The Devil's Dyke, where I met keen cyclists fixing their gears yet again. Of course I didn't put much strain on my three gears, as I always walked up hills. "You should be banned" they said as I coolly admired the hedge-top views from my sedate 'sit up and beg machine'.

I loved cycling east to west in Belsize, where the roads are flat, and don't often attempt the hill to the north. What excuse could I think of for continuing this happy and healthy lifestyle? Becoming a networker for AgeUK was the answer, in doing the rounds of the housebound, playing board games with them and imparting information.

Now I justify my cycling by visiting home-bound neighbours and giving out useful information. I am a networker in the community, but remember I'm just gathering information to pass on and don't have to join everything myself.

KWITS, or 'Keep Wendy in this street' is a phrase that was invented by my neighbours in Parkhill Road who like to see me swanning off on my bicycle each day. They enjoy our gatherings in the front garden and don't want me to retreat to the care of my daughter.

How lucky I am!

Original iron steps to a garden on Parkhill Road

Rear garden view Parkhill Road

BELSIZE Remembered

# Bartrams Convent Hostel
## *Residence for Female Students*

The Sisters of Providence of the Immaculate Conception was founded in Belgium in 1833 for the instruction of children, the care of orphan asylums and the service of the sick and prisoners. By 1876 there were a hundred and fifty of these convents in Belgium, England, Italy and the United States.

The Order acquired part of the Bartrams estate on Hampstead Green around 1867 and opened a private boarding school for girls. Although the original building was bombed during the war the Bartrams Convent Hostel was rebuilt in the 1950s on the site in Rowland Hill Street before the construction of the Royal Free Hospital. The residence accommodated female students in a simple but comfortable environment with shared bathroom and dining facilities. The hostel was maintained by the Sisters of Providence but females of all religions and beliefs were welcome.

The accommodation was considered ideal for students seeking independence while living in a friendly, peaceful residence. The former hostel was owned by the Convent for almost 50 years, but the Sisters sold the property and moved to a new home in Royston, Hertfordshire.

The sculpture on the front of the building was by Michael Werner who lived in Parliament Hill. Sadly it was discarded during the demolition of the building during November 2015.

Bartrams Convent Hostel before demolition

Michael Werner's statue, discarded
*Photo: Dr Paul Knight*

# HAVERSTOCK HILL AND EAST OF IT

Bartrams Convent Hostel, adjacent to the Royal Free, featured a 21ft high sculpture by Michael Werner
*Photo: Ranee Barr*

BELSIZE Remembered

# Market Gardens of Belsize
## *Helen Pollock*

On a map of Belsize around 1800 you would have seen few houses but fields, ponds and woodlands, and market gardens to feed Londoners with cabbages and early peas, manured with horse dung and night soil from the growing metropolis. From the mid 17th century intensive gardening in London's environs was spurred on by a fashion among the rich for a wide range of vegetables in their diet, which was copied by the middle classes. By the 1870s the farms and large country estates had given way to strings of terraced houses, and market gardens were being sold as building land.

No.116 Haverstock Hill, opposite England's Lane

Behind the houses on Haverstock Hill were the glass greenhouses of a 'new plant merchant', who specialised in greenhouse plants and in pelargoniums, fuchsias, and verbenas. He later grew orchids, and his annual orchid exhibition became one of the sights of the London season.

The landscape of the past haunts the present, for in the 1950s Geoffrey Gilbert, a journalist and commercial photographer, grew ferns and stocked his garden at No.116 Haverstock Hill with rare trees and plants. In 1968, his *Lazy Gardener's Guide* was available in the Belsize Bookshop at 193 Haverstock Hill.

The Manor of Belsize in 1814

HAVERSTOCK HILL AND EAST OF IT

Before construction of Belsize Park Underground station, this location looked rather different
John Russell Nurseries traded here for many decades, c.1910, *archive*

Salmon Florist traded at the Russell Nurseries site for over 40 years until 2012

BELSIZE Remembered

# Saving Belsize Woods
## *Friends of Belsize Wood*

Forming part of the Hampstead Ridge, a stretch of sloping woodland to the east of Haverstock Hill was the property of the Midland Railway Company in the 1860s. A railway tunnel runs beneath the woods. British railways leased the land for 21 years from 1948 to John Russell (Hampstead) Ltd [p71] which developed it as a nursery garden, jazz club and public tennis courts as well as some light industry. The wooded area was not built upon.

Later owned by Camden, redevelopment had been under consideration from 1971 as the Council wanted the land for housing. In 1977 a public enquiry was opened and the inspector's report concluded that there should be a "reasonable element of recreational provision easily accessible to the public".

Camden recommenced its planning procedure in 1982. This prompted a vigorous and angry local campaign to save the site, which was now named "Belsize Wood" to benefit from the prestigious association with Belsize Park. Campaigning groups included the Belsize Conservation Area Advisory Committee, the Globe Lawn Tennis Club on the Russell Nurseries site as well as the Belsize Residents' Association.

A solution was reached and the woodland was divided into a fenced off "Woodland Nature Reserve" now Belsize Wood, and an open "Woodland Leisure Area" now Russell Nurseries Wood.

The Belsize Woods were saved. A picturesque pathway of descending steps now runs through the deeply-shaded wooded areas populated with oaks, ashes, sycamore and holly trees with a very large oak tree in the southeast corner just down from the outdoor classroom. There is also a pond, a large insect house, bird boxes and a bird feeding area. The woods enjoy a broad diversity of insect species.

These woods occupy perhaps the last strip of indige-

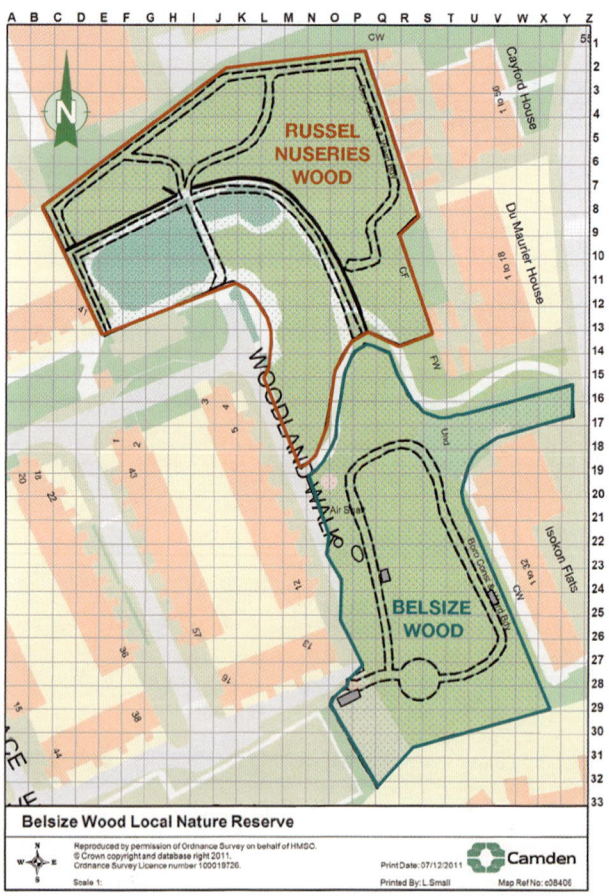

Belsize Woods Management Plan 2011 – Aspern Grove/Haverstock Hill are located to the west with Lawn Road to the east

nous woodland still remaining in the area, and thanks to the efforts of the conservationists and campaigners the woods have been preserved.

The Friends of Belsize Wood brings together people who work in the reserve and other local individuals with an interest in its management. Founded in 2004, the organisation has been particularly effective at raising grants to support development projects and site activities.

Belsize Wood is now protected as a Local Nature Reserve and a Site of Borough Importance for Nature Conservation, Grade II. And Russell Nurseries Woods is a Site of Nature Conservation Importance, Borough Grade II. Belsize Woods are within the Parkhill Conservation area and are open to the public every Saturday and Sunday during daylight hours. Russell Nurseries Woods are open during daylight hours every day. The woods can be accessed from Haverstock Hill via Aspern Grove, and the pathway leads down to Lawn Road.

Sources: D R Lawrence, Friends of Belsize Wood and the Belsize Woods Mgmt Plan, Nature for the Community, 2011

UCL Students, Belsize Wood, *photo: D Lawrence*

Morning in Belsize Wood

BELSIZE Remembered

# Downside Crescent, 1942-1999

## *Elizabeth Noyes*

I lived the first 57 years of my life in Downside Crescent, in a house bought by my grandmother in 1928. My parents were married in St Stephen's church.

Early memories are of the air raid shelters on the corner of Belsize Grove and Haverstock Hill. There was another one on the east side of Haverstock Hill, by what is now the entrance to the tennis club, outside what was then the post office. There were still bomb craters where some of the houses had been hit. As we were between the anti-aircraft gun emplacements on Primrose Hill and Parliament Hill our street suffered quite a lot of damage. There was a large patch on one of the bedroom walls where a wardrobe had been blown through in a raid. In the garden was a large piece of marble from a shop counter in Haverstock Hill that had come through the roof.

Two floors of the house were let out to All Hallows for a vicarage, as theirs had been bombed. I think my parents were slightly resentful of the fact that we were all on the second floor, while the vicar and his housekeeper had the other two floors. They moved out when I was about 11, so we got two floors, and two aunts came to live with us as well.

I was born in the war and although I cannot consciously remember it, the sound of an air raid siren, or fighter plane still make me stiffen. A response I must have learnt from my mother. Apparently much of the time I was kept under the sofa for safety.

There were two delicatessen shops in Haverstock Hill with strange smells and foods I was not used to. The people in there often spoke German. My father knew some German as he was in charge of firefighters in the area, many of whom were Jewish refugees. His German was therefore rather limited as to how to put out fires, not so useful when on holiday in Germany! I can remember most of the other shops as well. There was a Mac Fisheries where they made beautiful patterns with the fish. There were two Sainsbury shops. One was for meat, with one counter for fresh meat, the other for bacon etc. The other shop was for groceries with four counters.

Downside Crescent, 2007, *photo: Tony Kerpel*

You had to queue up at each one you wanted items from. At the cheese counter they had great cheeses that they cut with a wire. At the butter counter they took the amount of butter you wanted off a large pile and patted it into shape. Nearly everything, rice etc., had to be weighed out by hand. My sister and I liked the sweet shop next to the cinema best, where we took our pocket money and of course the coupon required when buying sweets.

Our fruit and vegetables came from Mr Rodd's(?) shop in Fleet Road, who delivered the goods ordered. Once a mouse was in the box and ran up my mother's arm. Bread came from Molls, also in Fleet Road. At the side was a mews with a dairy and they kept cows there.

Everyone walked to school and lived nearby. There was quite a stir when someone arrived in a car. Our parents saw us across Haverstock Hill, as there was no crossing then, and we then walked on our own.

Cressy Road Tram Depot, *archive*

In the bad winter of 1946/47 my father bought a sledge, as I kept falling in the snow and got cold and wet. We went to church in St Saviour's, Eton Road and could sledge down Haverstock Hill, as it was impassable to cars.

Trams and later trolley buses came up Fleet Road and were garaged in Cressy Road. Opposite was a paper factory. I think it was for recycling, as there were often little bits of paper in the road. In Lawn Road was a rag factory where the flats are now. One day it caught fire and there were rats running down the street.

Apart from playing at friends' houses and going to church, Hampstead Heath was the place of most recreation. We walked there often, flew kites, had our birthday parties there and in summer went to the lido. Often there also seemed to be gatherings in the home of Dr Fletcher at 166 Haverstock Hill. His daughter had married a Czech airman, who we thought was very exotic.

We had many visitors, a tradition started by my grandmother. When people came home on leave from the colonies we were allowed to stay up and listen to stories of far flung places.

About 1950 my father bought a car from a friend who was going abroad. It was one of the first in the road. It had to be parked facing the way of the traffic and if the lights were not on when it got dark a policeman would ring at the door to remind us.

I had to travel by Underground to my secondary school, so my friends lived outside the area and I went elsewhere for recreation.

My parents got married in 1941. No white dresses then as clothes were rationed. When I was aged two I had fur mittens and a bonnet. These were made out of rabbit fur, as my grandfather in Somerset used to trap rabbits and send them to us. This was good meat as well and was a welcome arrival until one rabbit got lost in the post for some weeks, and had to be rapidly buried as the smell was so bad. He also sent us tins of honey from his bees.

My other grandmother lived in Hertfordshire and kept chickens, so we used to walk to Finchley Road station (no 268 then) and go on the Metropolitan line to visit her and collect precious eggs. The war ration was one egg per person per week from the shops.

We walked to Finchley Road to go swimming in the old swimming baths opposite the end of College Crescent.

We were lucky in that my father was very practical. Coming from a tailoring family he made clothes for my sister and me out of scraps of cloth and my Mother's cut-down clothes. He also made my toys. There were no dolls, but I had a soft rabbit, which I still have. He also made little chairs and a table out of a packing case that survived for his grandchildren to use.

There were certain disadvantages to being practical. For months my mother had been saving up ingredients to make my father a birthday cake. Unfortunately after baking it proved to be inedible as she had used my father's toothpaste powder that he kept in an old flour bag. The dried fruit had to be washed out for reuse. Another time my father built a meat safe to put on the window ledge to keep food cool, as there were no fridges. I crawled inside and got stuck, so the whole thing had to be dismantled.

BELSIZE Remembered

# Downside Crescent, 1907-2007
## *Tony Kerpel*

A few years ago Camden Council notified residents that it wanted to resurface Downside Crescent and that meant that residents had to remove their cars for one day. It so happens that I had collected photographs of the street from 1907 and thought that this work would present a unique opportunity to compare the street as it had been and 100 years later.

Apart from a few different lamp posts and notices detailing parking restrictions it would be easy to confuse the two scenes. Looking at the photographs you can see that little has changed, the basic structures and frontages of the houses have remained the same. This is primarily because the local council has prevented owners from concreting over front gardens to park their cars as well as preventing dormer windows from being put into loft conversions.

Downside Crescent, 1907, *archive photo supplied by T Kerpel*

Downside Crescent in 2007, *photo: T Kerpel*

BELSIZE Remembered

# The Spies of Lawn Road & the Lawn Road Flats
## *Gene Adams*

Between the wars, Belsize Park became rundown, and was even known as 'poor man's Hampstead'. Being also charming, tree-lined and peaceful, despite the bombs during the war, the area designated today as the Parkhill Conservation Area attracted a group of young artists looking for lodgings in buildings with large rooms to adapt as studios. Henry Moore, Barbara Hepworth and Ben Nicholson were a few of the residents.

In the 1930s some of those fleeing Hitler, like Marcel Breuer and Walter Gropius, were in time to find flats with their friend Jack Pritchard in his newly-built startlingly 'modernist' Lawn Road Flats, now known as the Isokon building. The flats were built in 1934 by entrepreneur Jack Pritchard and designed by a talented young Canadian architect, Wells Coates (1898-1958). They exemplified a new social idea of a "machine for living" developed from the Bauhaus School in Berlin, closed down as one of the Nazi cultural targets.

The Isokon building
*Photo: Nicholas Kane*

Pro-Soviet Communism was thrown into disarray in August 1939 with the astonishing Nazi-Soviet Pact. Those devoting their lives to the fight against Fascism were suddenly expected to condone Hitler, leading some to resign from the Party. This impasse was resolved in a manner of speaking when Hitler treacherously invaded Russia in 1941, omitting to inform Stalin in spite of their previous 'pact'. The Nazi use of brutal force against the beleaguered Russian people shocked Churchill and the Allies. They joined forces with Stalin to defeat the German attack, despite their distrust of Communism.

Many of the refugees were Jewish intellectuals and ardent Communists, the Party being at that time the only effective organised opposition to racist Fascism, which had become the official creed of Nazi Germany, and later Italy. Naturally, 'comrades' in the UK were ready to help refugees. Some were found lodgings in the unfashionable old Victorian houses, by then divided into flats or bedsits.

Among them was the Kuczynski family, "a highly educated and gifted German-Polish Jewish family… already involved with the British and German Communist Parties," says Dr David Burke, the Cambridge historian, in his second study of Soviet espionage in this part of Belsize Park.

Dr Klaus Fuchs

Kim Philby, Soviet stamp

Professor Jürgen Kuczynski

Ursula Kuczynski, age 20

Ursula Kuczynski (1907-2003), one of the professor's daughters, who used several other cover names, also became the handler of the more notorious Klaus Fuchs, and was herself regarded by her Russian spymasters with great admiration, to the point of becoming an honorary Red Army Colonel and nicknamed "Red Sonya".

In 1977 as 'Ruth Werner', living her last years in East Berlin, she wrote an absolutely riveting autobiography describing her life as a spy during the pre-digital age; safe houses, carbon copies, hollow tree trunks, amateur radio transmissions and all that. Her book gave a detailed description of her parents' "dowdy three roomed flat in NW3", in Lawn Road, when her artist mother "cooked the way she painted in a kitchen full of inspired disorder" – just like their grand house in Schlachtensee, Berlin, from which they had fled. It is hard to believe that during that time there were "no less than thirty two agents or subagents connected to Soviet espionage associated with the Lawn Road Flats" and with a few older houses nearby. Some are notorious, like Klaus Fuchs, Arnold Deutsch and Kim Philby; others have remained secret until now.

Dr Burke knits together an illuminating context of social history with the sudden dawn in Lawn Road of Modernism which was "unquestionably the architecture of the Progressives; it had its economic and social origins in 1930s Political and Economic Planning and had a lineage going back to the Arts and Crafts Movement of William Morris at the end of the nineteenth century." Wells Coates' striking design was understandably strange and alarming to the natives in 1934 but is now our most distinguished Grade I listed 20th century building in Belsize Park, conserved by numerous local and national campaigns, and restored after forty years of neglect. Isokon, as we now call it (from Isometric Unit Constructions), is once more a worthy object of pilgrimage for the dozens of students and tourists who stand on the pavement outside and gaze admiringly upwards at the edge of Molly and Jack Pritchard's splendid sundeck on the roof.

Sources: *The Spy Who Came In From the Co-op*, David Burke, Boydell & Brewer, 2008
*The Lawn Road Flats: Spies, Writers and Artists*, David Burke, Boydell & Brewer, 2014
*Sonya's Report*, Ruth Werner, Chatto & Windus in English, 1991
*The Belsize Story* Vol 2, David S Percy, Aulis Productions, 2013

BELSIZE Remembered

# Rescuing Numbers 104-110 Haverstock Hill

*Helen Pollock*

Lower down Haverstock Hill from the basement garden flat at No.186 where I used to live were four houses numbered 104 to 110. They had stood empty, with the exception of a few stubborn tenants, after Camden Council compulsorily purchased them for redevelopment in the early 1970s. They were beginning to crumble, with large cracks in the walls and iron pins.

They had sizable overgrown front gardens and red, black and white chequered tiling leading to the steps up to the front door. At a time when No.186 Haverstock Hill was under pressure from a Charlotte Street agent to morph into a hotel, all the then tenants (including me) had gone down to No.106 to see if it could be a squat. We found the house redeemable for habitation although Council workers had superficially trashed it to make it less attractive to squatting. The lavatories had been filled with cement and smashed, and the wiring had been cut and left trailing.

One of us had gone up into the attic and found the electrics left in working condition and in principle the whole house could be run from there. The guttering had been pulled away, but the wisteria climbing all over the front of the house in a great beautiful tangle of curling fronds and dripping bunches of pale blue flowers still supported the disconnected down pipes. The steps from the ground floor into the basement had been destroyed. The kitchen had a stove and a double ceramic Belfast butler sink which had not been touched. The kitchen door opened to the side of the hill and had lost the five or six steps down into the garden, a tangled growth which nevertheless included a pear and an apple tree and raspberry bushes, nettles and wild blackberries, the ghost of a pond and a kitchen garden.

The verdict was that if 'push came to shove' it would be possible to restore services and make good. Six months later we were able to help friends to move into this house as they were going to be evicted from their squats in Prince of Wales Road. The local authority was busy building housing estates at the expense of the local community and the eclectic mix of factories, small manufacturing industries, such as an ice cream factory, clothing and paint manufacturers, piano factories and rows of workers' two-up, two-down terraces.

Eventually, as is commonly known, the houses were restored to their former high-Victorian glory instead of being replaced by a modern, characterless box.

Nos.104-110 Haverstock Hill in 2016

Pathway leading to No.106 Haverstock Hill

# Steven Spielberg comes to Belsize
## *Lester Hillman*

The Screen on the Hill, our local cinema on Haverstock Hill in the 1990s, on occasion itself delivered drama fit for the big screen. On the evening of Sunday 27 June 1999 the Screen on the Hill was the venue for a London film preview of *The Last Days* (1998) organised by the Spiro Institute. The film focuses on the plight of five Hungarian Jews who survived imprisonment in Auschwitz when the Nazis began to exterminate Hungarian Jews.

Among those present at the screening was 75-year old Holocaust survivor Renee Firestone, over from her home in the United States. Also from the States was Steven Spielberg, Executive Producer of *The Last Days*, winner of an Oscar in 1999 for the Best Documentary. It was a production by the Shoah Foundation which came out of Spielberg's film *Schindler's List* released in 1993.

At 8pm that Sunday evening Steven Spielberg was in evidence to the crowds gathered outside the cinema. Reports from the time also mention Richard Dreyfuss and Olympia Dukakis also present, helping to support the preview event.

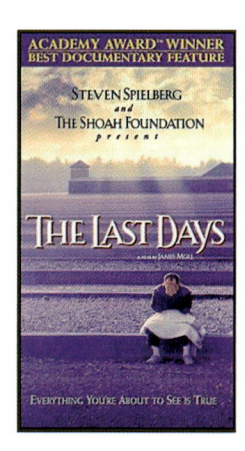

The Screen on the Hill – now the Everyman Belsize Park
*Photo: Philip Grey*

BELSIZE Remembered

# Wartime in and Around Parkhill Road

*Margaret Pennell*

I grew up in the 1930s in a block of flats in Garnett Road. Although just a small child I enjoyed playing with friends who also lived in the block. Our simple games included playing in the road using the lamp posts (with three chalked stripes) as a wicket. We were rarely interrupted by passing cars. We also played chasing in the 'Chinese alleys'. These were the fenced back paths into the rear of the new houses in Upper Park Road, Garnett Road and Parkhill Road. Next to these houses between Upper Park Road and Parkhill Roads were some large Victorian artists' studios.

When my mother took me to the Parkhill Road Studios I remember being impressed with their enormous size – double height rooms, each with a very large window.

Sometimes we also played in the creepy tree-lined drive of the Fever Hospital in Lawn Road. Next to the hospital there was a sawmill and in the summer the distant sound of the saw produced a lovely lazy background.

On Saturdays we went to the children's pictures for 3d at the Odeon Haverstock Hill, and on sunny summer days we would go over to play on the Heath for hours at a time.

When I was about eight I was introduced to the Belsize Library on Antrim Road and I obtained my own library ticket. I loved the place; it was large and light with its big windows, bright oak furniture and bookshelves. Sometimes my father, a keen cyclist, took me in his sidecar to St Pancras to see the working horses stabled under the arches.

I went to Fleet Road school and in the summer the Wall's 'Stop me and buy one' tricycle was often parked outside when we came out of school. My favourite cost a penny, but I was often able to buy half for a ha'penny.

I remember before the war there were three local sweet shops just around the corner from our flat in Garnett Road. One stocked sweets at a farthing, a ha'penny, and a penny plus more expensive ones at 2d and 3d.

Then in September 1939 war was declared. I was evacuated to Berkhamsted but after a few months returned to Belsize as it had become quieter on the home front in London. One night I was woken up with a loud bang and glass showered over my bed from the window. A landmine had been dropped between Parkhill and

Parkhill Road Studios, 1880, *archive*

Upper Park Roads. The next morning my mother and I went to look at the damage. Several houses in Parkhill Road and the artists' studios had been completely demolished. After that we regularly spent our nights in an air raid shelter. Four shelters had been built in the once empty yard on the corner of Garnett Road and Upper Park Road. They were furnished with bunk beds and presumably had lavatories. My mother had the bottom bunk and I the top.

Then my father who fire watched got called up and I insisted we left London to be safe. After a while my mother decided she wanted to be back home and so we returned in the midst of the continuing Blitz of London. Because our spaces in the shelter had been taken my mother decided we should go up to Belsize Park tube. As we ventured outside the world around us was exploding, bombs were dropping, anti-aircraft guns were firing, and the entire sky was bright red from burning fires. It was the most frightening experience. Arm in arm we hurried up Downshire Hill. We got as far as the deep air raid shelter on the corner of Haverstock Hill and we looked back down the hill to see the black silhouette of the dome of St Paul's Cathedral surrounded by a sweeping search light.

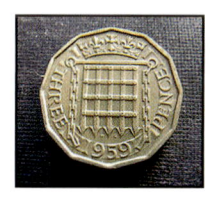

On Fridays my friends and I would go to the fish and chips shop in Fleet Road and we treated ourselves to a thru'penny bag of chips and a thru'penny bottle of Tizer.

On Saturdays mother and I would go to the pictures at the Odeon cinema Haverstock Hill, or to the cinema on South End Green.

When the war ended Garnett Road celebrated with huge bonfires in the middle of the road. There were people from all around singing and dancing and being very happy; until a big spout of water erupted in the middle of the fire which had burnt through the road surfacing and burst the pipe underneath.

In 1947 I left home.

I returned in 1964 to live in a bedsitter in Adelaide Road and now my nearest shops were in England's Lane. There was a bank on the corner and a proper ironmonger. A few yards along there was a dairy. After a while I moved into my own home on Haverstock Hill in 1975, and once again I was reunited with my beloved library in Antrim Road. St Mary's Maternity Hospital was at the corner of Belsize Grove. On Haverstock Hill was a small J. Sainsbury – the grocery shop, then further along was another Sainsbury – the butchers and poulterers. Just beyond Howitt Road was a fish and chips shop. The Odeon had disappeared and been replaced by the smaller Screen on the Hill and Budgens supermarket. On the other side of the road the main post office remained. Next to it was Sonia Very Ladies Fashions – later to be replaced by the Victoria Wine shop. Further down by Belsize Park tube station was the florist and plant shop. Russell Nurseries had been replaced by Salmon Florist. The Nurseries themselves had been replaced by tennis courts. My nightmare deep shelter had become an archive storage facility. Many of the shops have changed but the wide tree-lined pavements have not, and the area is still 'my Belsize' – la belle isle indeed.

Original iron balconet
Parkhill Road

BELSIZE Remembered

# Belsize Fire Station 1915-2014
## Tim Lamden

Belsize Fire Station was designed by the Fire Brigade branch of the London County Council (LCC) Architects Department. Building work began on the station in Lancaster Grove, Belsize Park, in 1912 and on 22 May 1915 the station was officially opened by Percy C Simmons, chairman of the LCC's Fire Brigade Committee.

It was listed Grade II* by English Heritage, which described it as "One of the most distinctive and original of a remarkable series of fire stations built by the LCC between 1896-1914".

Fire crews worked through two world wars, remaining operational throughout the Blitz of London from 1940 to 1941. Crews at Belsize attended the 1987 King's Cross fire and the 7/7 bombings in 2005. In January 2012, the crew at Belsize helped save hundreds of lives during a blaze at Taplow tower block in Swiss Cottage.

The station was closed permanently in January 2014 as part of London-wide fire station closures enforced by Mayor of London Boris Johnson in a bid to save £29 million. Many bitter tears were shed over this draconian overruling of strong local feeling. Campaigners have argued that the building was not fit for any other purpose, due to its unique design, but in fact there is a plan to convert the listed building into apartments.

In June 2017 a property development company received consent from the Camden planning department to convert the fire station into 16 flats with two affordable homes.

Based on a January 2014
*Ham&High* article by Tim Lamden
Updated 2017

The Grade II*-listed Belsize Fire Station is a very clever interpretation of an Arts and Crafts-style house, adapted for the fire brigade. With its highly-visible tower, the fire station is by LCC Architect Charles Canning Winmill.

The wonderful Belsize Fire Station was designed by somebody who was very close to Philip Webb who is the most Arts and Crafts architect ever. It is one of the few fire stations known to have been designed by Charles Canning Winmill himself.

Professor Andrew Saint – *The Belsize Story*

IMPORTANT BUILDINGS

Belsize Fire Station
Lancaster Grove, c.1969, *archive*

Belsize Fire Station – still operational in 2012

85

BELSIZE Remembered

# Belsize Branch Library
## *Michael Gorman*

In 1958, I was assigned to be one of four junior assistants at the Belsize branch located in the corner where Antrim Road and Antrim Grove meet. The library was and is a striking modern single-storey building, designed by Gold and Aldridge and opened in March 1937. It consists, essentially, of one large, public room with a staff area attached. The Belsize branch was the site of an exciting technological innovation – photocharging.

Belsize Branch Library late 1930s, *RIBA archive*

Michael Gorman in Belsize Branch Library, 1958
*photo provided by M Gorman*

This was a book lending system that used a microfilm camera to photograph the "accession" (identifying) number of the book together with the borrower's card and linking the two with a punched "transaction" card that was inserted in a pocket of the book. When the book was returned the transaction cards were sorted – any missing cards identified books that were overdue. Sorting was achieved by the distinctly low-tech means of inserting long needles into the punched holes and allowing those that were notched at that number to fall off. Then one could take the list of missing numbers and scroll through the microfilm to locate the name and address of delinquent borrowers. I became quite adept in all aspects of photocharging, up to and including wielding the sorting needle, and was sent to demonstrate the (extremely simple) procedures when it was installed in the other branches.

I remember a pre-Christmas party in the Belsize Library in which we brought in food and drink and, after the doors were closed, ate, drank, and made merry to music from a tape player (the first time I had seen such a thing). I kissed all three of the young lady assistants at different times as the music played on and the evening turned to night and then to early morning. It was a high old time and the transgressive nature of holding the party on official premises, drinking and dancing, and holding long conversations in corners with the young ladies, until the pale light dawned over NW3 was an unmatched thrill.

I felt myself, for the first time, to be a true Hampstead bohemian, if only for a night, despite the essential innocence of the event.

IMPORTANT BUILDINGS

# The Belsize Library
## *Marion Hill*

It wasn't until 1998 that I worked at the Belsize Library in the newly-created role of Library Manager. My first task was to prepare the library for closure! But thankfully, on that occasion, the library was reprieved and given a new lease of life as the Friends and staff worked together to organise events and activities involving the local community as much as possible.

During my four years there we ran children's concerts, received a collection of books donated by Christians Together in Camden, welcomed Lauren Child who had chosen Belsize Library to receive £500 for books as part of her Kate Greenaway Medal prize, invited former library assistant Sarah Waters to read from her book *Fingersmith* short-listed for the Orange Prize, and hosted the Marylebone Birdwatching Society's 20th Anniversary party. This included the launch of its website, and we organised a series of displays. And although I was moved to a different library in the autumn of 2002, in October of that year we held the first meeting of the Belsize French Club [p46], which continues to meet at the library.

---

### Troublesome Eccentrics Plague Belsize Library

**Belsize branch library** in Antrim Road is plagued by "troublesome eccentrics" says the librarian in his annual report. They are monocled old men with long hair, dowdily-dressed middle-aged women and a few foreigners, who turn the once peaceful reading room into a rowdy house.

There is a time limit of 10 minutes on each of the periodicals and it is when readers keep them over the time limit that the rows begin. The "eccentrics" go up to offenders and complain, snatch the newspapers and magazines from one another, tearing them to shreds at times. They shout, swear and argue and sometimes nearly come to blows.

*Ham&High*, 2 August 1957

### Our Library – Listed At Last!

When I survey our Library
It seems more safely there
Because Those In Authority
Deem it worth love and care.

May it serve to delight us now
And many years to come:
A lovely, useful house that is
Leisure's and Learning's home!

Robert Ilson

BELSIZE Remembered

# St Peter's Church Belsize Square
## Alfonso Vonscheidt

I was brought to St Peter's Church in 1939 by my mother when I was six years old; we had just moved to London from Manchester, my father had died at the end of 1938.

The country was a bit of a mess because everybody knew there was going to be a war. I grew up with St Peter's as part of my life, but as I got older, I became disenchanted with St Peter's as there were very few people of my own age. I wrote some letters to the local papers around 1952-1953, and this resulted in a phone call from someone who belonged to the Congregational Church opposite St Stephen's. He told me they had a Young People's Fellowship for 16 to 35-year-olds. I tried it out and started to make friends, so I decided to leave St Peter's and join Lyndhurst Road Congregational Church. I worshipped there for the next 19 years.

However, I rejoined St Peter's in 1972 when a new vicar, one Richard Truss, arrived. I have worshipped there ever since. I was soon put on the parochial church council and have always been a member except for one year; for twelve of those years I was churchwarden, most of the time with Richard and then with Donald Barnes.

Something amusing occurred one year at Easter, when Donald Barnes was vicar. I got myself to church on Easter Sunday with a very heavy cold; I only went because it was Easter. I said to Donald, "I think I will take Communion right at the end, so as not to pass germs on to anybody else". So I did that, and Donald said, "Will you finish off the wine?" When I got back to my pew I was so drunk that I couldn't stand up when the service finished! I managed to make somebody aware of my condition, and he brought me a strong cup of coffee. I leant against one of the pillars for a while so that it looked as if I was all right but I had to stay like that for half an hour. I had visions of headlines in the *News of the World*: 'Churchwarden Drunk at Easter Sunday Service'!

In 1972 the local Liberal Party got wind of a plan by the then Heath government to extend the M1 and build a motorway ring road around central London. This would have destroyed Belsize Park. Everything between Swiss Cottage and Haverstock Hill would have been flattened including St Peter's. There were petitions and a lot of hostilities, but with the change of government the plan was scrapped in 1974.

I naturally made many friends at St Peter's over the years, and learned that it's impossible to overestimate the value of prayer. During the Second World War, a book was published called *Britain's Secret Weapon*, and that weapon was Prayer. I think it's a great title.

Based on an interview with Peter Roscoe

St Peter's Belsize Square, c.1905, *archive*

IMPORTANT BUILDINGS

# The Vicarage, Belsize Square

*Veronica Jupp Veasey*

We moved to Belsize Square in the early 1950s when I was ten. My father was vicar of St Peter's Church and the old redbrick vicarage, which was in a dilapidated state, had been sold to the new Belsize Square Synagogue [p90].

A replacement vicarage had just been built next to the church [p11]. It was designed by the architect Leslie Wood and seemed to be very modern indeed. My mother and older sister had fun choosing 'modern' curtain material from Heal's for the large square sliding metal windows and the two French doors. My father then set about creating a haphazard but exuberant garden in the waste ground that remained. He was often out in the garden contemplating his plants, or possibly future sermons, and chatting over the fence to passers by.

At that time Belsize Square was shabby, with peeling paintwork, the houses divided into bedsits, and not a car to be seen. But it was full of interesting people, as it is today.

Completed in 1953, St Peter's third vicarage with its large ground floor rear windows

BELSIZE Remembered

# Belsize Square Synagogue

*Antony Godfrey*

The early congregation was predominantly made up of German Jews from Berlin and Frankfurt. The synagogue officially started in 1939, with the first service taking place on the 24th March of that year. Meetings were initially held at No.27 Belsize Park, opposite St Peter's Church on Belsize Square. At first there was no formal congregational organisation and each service was conducted by a different rabbi and cantor, recently arrived in the UK. Later in 1951, the former vicarage of St Peter's was acquired and converted to accommodate a modest synagogue seating 80, with communal offices, and a religion school. This soon proved to be inadequate for the huge membership. So an extension was built and finally completed in June 1958.

It was a Bauhaus-style construction that shocked some members who were expecting a more traditional synagogue. In recent times refurbishments have created the modern, beautiful and inspiring synagogue we know today. Now, the sanctuary and synagogue hall can hold more than a thousand people, uniting the community under one roof.

The Belsize Square Synagogue is distinguished by its music – we have an organ and a full choir. The music is 19th-century German Romantic.

The old synagogue is now part of the new synagogue on high holidays and festivals.

Antony Godfrey is author of *Three Rabbis in a Vicarage*
Larsen Grove Press, 2005

No. 27 Belsize Park where meetings were held initially

Belsize Square Synagogue entrance

IMPORTANT BUILDINGS

Frontage of the Belsize Square Synagogue previously St Peter's second vicarage

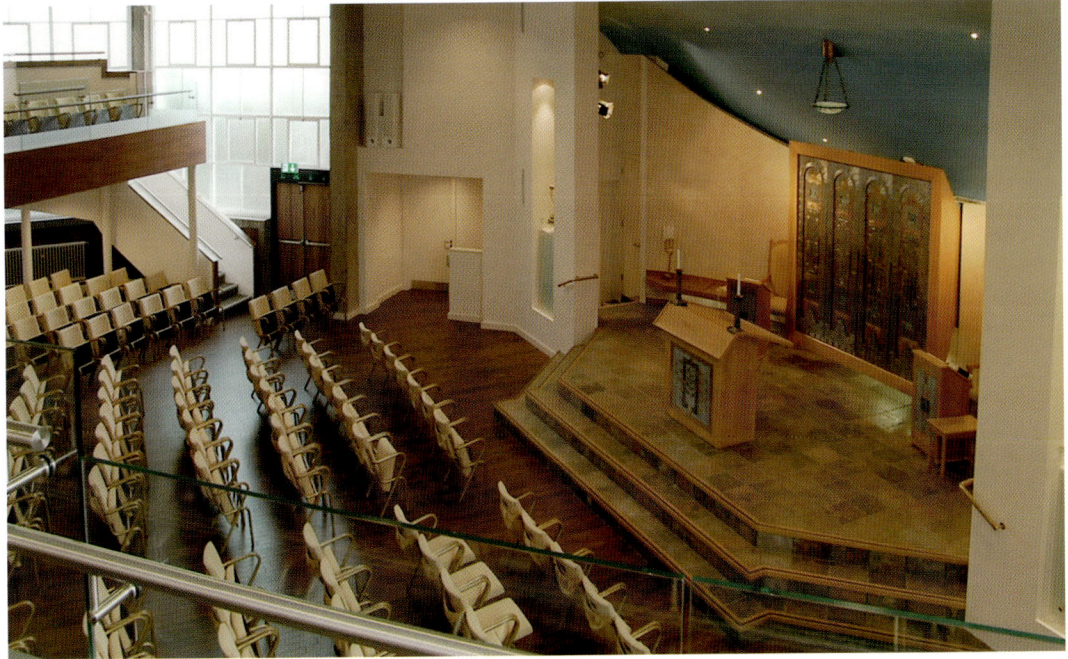

Interior of the 1958 Bauhaus-style extension to the Belsize Square Synagogue

BELSIZE Remembered

# Belsize Park Station
## *Grade II-listed*

**M**any London Underground stations have a unique architectural style, and English Heritage considers that this should be respected and recognised.

English Heritage Chief Executive Simon Thurley said on 26 July 2011, "The stations awarded listed status today are as valuable to London's architectural story as many more famous buildings like the Houses of Parliament." He called Belsize Park tube station "distinctive and instantly recognizable" with the "glazed façades of the early 20th century stations… It is absolutely right that these stations be offered the recognition and protection offered by listing."

Although listing won't prevent the stations from being changed in the future, it does mean that any upgrades will have to take into account the station's history and heritage. This measure should ensure that the station continues to look the way it does for a long time to come.

Expert Gareth Edwards said, "Belsize Park has the iconic red façade that can be seen on stations throughout the city. This is the work of Leslie Green, who designed over 50 stations in just four years. Green was under orders to make his stations distinctive but cheap, and at only 9 shillings (45p) a foot, the red fronting did exactly that."

The station includes a Second World War air raid shelter

Platform ticket

Belsize Park Underground station c.1910, *archive*

IMPORTANT BUILDINGS

*Leslie Green's distinctive Belsize Park station set back from the road with the Underground roundel in the forecourt*

which could accommodate 8,000 people in two giant tunnels. This is one of eight London Underground stations that have deep-level air-raid shelters underneath them – used these days for storage. The shelter entrance is located at the top of Downside Crescent.

Belsize Park station is on a line that is the result of the merger of two companies. The first was the City & South London Railway, opened in 1890. It was London's first deep-level tube railway, and the first to be operated by electric locomotives. Then, 1907 saw the opening of a second line, running from Charing Cross via Camden Town, which was known as The Hampstead Tube. When connected to the City & South London Railway it became today's Northern Line in the 1920s.

BELSIZE Remembered

# The Christian Community Church on Glenilla Road
*Mona Bradley with Andrew Welburn*

Does No.32 really shine out from Glenilla Road or is it just in my memory? At any rate, many residents of Belsize will have a passing acquaintance with the little church and its radiant, light-filled and also musically friendly space. Over many years it stood, together with the house (No.34), as the centre in Britain of a lively and expanding cultural-religious movement. From here that movement sowed seeds in the English-speaking countries around the world, seeds which continue to flourish and grow. But also it was always intensely local: local people came here to meet each other, as well as internationally-acclaimed musicians, like the Endellion Quartet, or actresses such as Sybil Thorndike, who on occasion graced its events. Those were on top of the stream of christenings, communions, weddings, funerals and memorial services, which always spilled over in happy crowds onto the pavement outside.

Locals must have noted these happy gatherings, especially when one day the *Ham&High* reported the opening of our clubroom with a silver key by the Mayor, Lieutenant- Colonel H Ashley-Scarlett, to be graciously thanked by Lady Pratt; perhaps that was when we 'arrived' in the district. But more than anything they flocked to our pioneer Advent markets. All it needed back in 1966 was 'a couple of thousand attractive leaflets put into the innumerable letterboxes in the immediate vicinity', and people came; and they came back – well, quite a few of them. That was, perhaps, because what they found assembled on the stalls was not jumble but people's love and enthusiasm. Tea and cakes devotedly made which, someone said, actually tasted of love and enthusiasm.

I was there for quite a while as secretary to the leading spirit behind the church's life and activities, Dr Alfred Heidenreich. Others who helped make it all happen were figures such as Karola Hart, and Elisabeth Scharff, still remembered today. Karola was German-born but English-

The Church of the Christian Community, Glenilla Road, 2011

married, though she came to us only in 1948, with her mother, to work for the Christian Community. Her obituary (1969) says she was an institution, which may sound a chilling word but in those days it meant 'very prized indeed'. She dealt with reminders, tax-refunds, minutes and agendas for us, but always humanised and embellished the squareness of the printed programmes by writing The Christian Community in large flowing lettering by hand over the top. 'Scharffie' had been a nurse who managed to get her Jewish patients out of Germany, only to find herself closed down in England by a fearful government. Medical and religious interests brought her to us, and her guaranteed twenty cakes were a centrepiece of the Advent market stalls, amongst which one year she dramatically collapsed and died.

Musical highlights included the first performance in Britain of the rarely heard Biber *Mysteries*, sonatas keyed to the meditative imagery of Christian devotion, in 1957. More aggressively modern works predominated in the church's hosting of the Hampstead Festival of 1961, when the TES reviewer noted that the Glenilla Arts Group 'bravely' offered

Stravinsky and Lennox Berkeley as well as some of their own compositions, but he may possibly have preferred the 'superb' renderings of Mozart and Schubert, or Bernard Roberts' Beethoven Recital ('his interpretation is something to be reckoned with').

Drama was hard-hitting too: parricide and incest in the suburbs of NW3 with a new translation of *Oedipus the King*, which the reviewer said 'carried conviction' and impressed with its symbolic gestures of sacrifice and denunciation. Sybil Thorndike had spoken there just the previous year about the role of Lady Macbeth, adding that to her, acting was a sort of 'sacred calling' and that when taking the role of such terrible characters she inwardly held on to a sense of God looking down and pitying them. Drama and music have always continued in the church, with Claire Rauter's eversure hand in finding and fostering new musical talents as well as inviting the old – maintained right up to her death.

The inside of the church contains some unexpected treasures. On the back wall are stone bas-relief panels portraying the Baptism and Crucifixion among seven scenes from the life of Christ. They were made around 1952 by Annabel Sprigge, an artist who belonged to the congregation, and achieve a powerful religious statement precisely through her creative freedom from literalness and reportage. They 'project into space what belongs together in time', so that spirit and meaning predominate over outer event, following the emphasis of the Christian Community movement and Rudolf Steiner, its inspiring teacher.

Looking back in 1958, ten years after the Church was consecrated, Dr Heidenreich referred to Steiner as 'a man sent from God'; to many of us Dr Heidenreich himself appeared in a rather similar light. He spoke and wrote tirelessly to further religious renewal after the awful time of the war. The movement itself had sprung to life, as he recalled, from an 'unusual gathering of people' back in 1922. The founding forty-five members were a diverse group. They no longer saw it as the church's task to instruct through sermons, but focused on the sacraments which hold life together in its many aspects: 'an experience worth going to church for, because the presence of the Living Christ is assuredly not transmitted by mechanical waves'. Their church was not based on signing people up to certain beliefs or upholding conventional formulae: starting from the sacramental experience, priests and congregation can freely explore and seek to understand the religious traditions and history of the past, while equally concerned with looking to the future. From its outset the Christian Community recognised the equal role of women and men in all aspects of that undertaking.

In 1948 some of those high ideals were inscribed on a vellum scroll which was laid beneath the threshold of the still incomplete new building. There was music (Bach), of course, and for the priests Adam Bittleston spoke of 'the earnestness of our task of building a church into which so many young people would come and receive vital impressions an impulses for their lives.' The architect Kenneth Bayes was present, along with his little daughter, who found the occasion on a windswept January day rather draughty and exclaimed accusingly, 'Daddy hasn't put the roof on!'

By June the roof was on, though the striking speciallycarved entrance door had to be held back till September. But no one waited for that. The June dedication and first act of consecration in the new church brought an overflowing crowd of 240 people, and in the afternoon there were two christenings and a wedding, followed by marionettes for the children (but not Punch and Judy). Greetings and good wishes came in from the overall leader of the movement in Stuttgart, Dr Emil Bock, and from the Christian Community in Czechoslovakia, in Scandinavia, and the congregations in England and Scotland. Dr Heidenreich gave the Dedication Address, 'to anchor, as it were, the new building spiritually in the widths of space and the depths of time'. 'Now,' he added, 'in this qualitative space-time this new church will stand and speak the quiet message of its presence through its created form.' It still speaks quietly though radiantly to many about a different side of life to that which surges and bustles so strongly through the capital.

The Christian Community has more recently built elsewhere, and its future at No.32 Glenilla Road is uncertain, but many of us hope that its message will continue to reach gently, luminously to those who come there.

*Information, dates and quotations taken from the Christian Community Journal for the relevant year*

BELSIZE Remembered

# Hampstead Town Hall

*Helen Marcus*

The Hampstead Vestry Hall was constructed on the corner of Haverstock Hill and Belsize Avenue, after the division in 1873 of the old parish of Hampstead into wards and the doubling of the number of vestrymen to 60. The London County Council was formed in 1888 when Hampstead parish ceased to be in Middlesex and became part of London, and in 1900 the vestries became borough councils with new powers and statutory duties. So the Vestry Hall became the Hampstead Town Hall.

Another Local Government re-organisation in 1964 saw the end of Hampstead Borough Council, when it was merged with St Pancras and part of Holborn to become part of the London Borough of Camden.

The new Camden Council was keen to destroy the feeling of Hampstead as a distinct community and wanted to demolish the Town Hall and replace it with council housing. Locals were up in arms. First, the South End Green Association had it Listed Grade II. Then the Heath & Hampstead Society brought together a host of local organizations to form a combined action group, the Friends of Hampstead Town Hall, in an attempt to save the building.

Hampstead Vestry Hall, Haverstock Hill c.1878, *archive*

The Town Hall in 2012

Camden Councillor John Mills helped the Friends to obtain a stay of six months to come up with a viable use for the Hall, at the same time pointing out that a worthy organisation in Kentish Town called InterChange which supported disabled and disadvantaged young people with talent in performing arts was in need of larger premises and had already had their eye on the old Town Hall. The National Lottery had just started, the profits from which were to be directed towards community projects and the conservation of heritage property. Successful applications were made to the Heritage Lottery Fund on account of the building and from the Arts Council Lottery Fund to support InterChange, to a total of between six and seven million pounds. The Friends of Hampstead Town Hall raised £70,000 as their share of match funding and also secured more by way of 'in kind' donations.

Our researches into the history of the building discovered that Joseph Joachim, Brahms' favourite violinist had played there in the 1890s. Part of the fundraising campaign entailed performing exactly the same programme.

The building now has multiple community uses. One of the main occupants is Wac Arts (Weekend Arts College), formerly InterChange, with daily use of the recording studio, several performance spaces with seating and hearing loops, studios with sprung floors, sound-proof music rooms and

Helen Marcus greeting HRH the Prince of Wales at the re-opening on 11 July 2000

rehearsal spaces, specialist aerials rigging and equipment, portable sound systems, a digital arts studio, a music technology room, drama studio and sensory pod. Another major user is the University of the Third Age, and a host of local societies including the Belsize Residents' Association use its committee room for their meetings. Altogether, a heartening story.

Helen Marcus, formerly chair, Friends of Hampstead Town Hall
Additional information, Celia Greenwood, CEO, Wac Arts

BELSIZE Remembered

# Lyndhurst Gardens
## *Corinne Gibbons*

Numbers 22, 24 and 26 Lyndhurst Gardens were built by William Willett and Sons. Harry Measures, one of several architects used by the Willetts, was a keen designer of billiard rooms, which is why my sitting room on the ground floor overlooking the garden at the rear of the house has three steps down to a central rectangular area where a billiard table would have been located.

These three houses were built for multiple occupancy, although in the 1890s that would have meant that the top floors were occupied by the servants!

Many of the houses in Lyndhurst Gardens were speculatively built and actually remained empty for quite some time after they were completed.

The properties have retained many of their delightful stained glass windows, another characteristic of the houses. One feature of our part of the house is not original: we have a pair of Adam doors that were made for a library at No.33 or No.35 Rosslyn Hill, both purchased by my father in 1969. But the houses were sold to Camden Council in 1974 to be converted into flats. During the refurbishment the Adam library was dismantled, and to our horror, the best features were being put onto a bonfire in the back of the garden to be burnt. Fortunately, my father was able to rescue the doors which were brought to 22 Lyndhurst Gardens where he installed them and built bookshelves to match.

Nos.22 and 24 Lyndhurst Gardens and William Willett Jr

IMPORTANT BUILDINGS

A gryphon above No.26 Lyndhurst Gardens

Original stained glass windows in No.22 Lyndhurst Gardens

99

BELSIZE Remembered

# Saving St Stephen's
## *Michael Taylor*

This was a popular and physically sound church until in 1970 severe cracks started to appear in the fabric of the church. It was closed for worship in 1976. The agenda of the Diocese as far as we know was to do nothing with the building, let it collapse, and sell the land to the adjacent Royal Free Hospital as a car park. English Heritage then pressed the Diocese on its legal responsibility to find a sensible use for the edifice. As a result my wife and I were invited to a meeting at Diocesan House, and the St Stephen's Restoration and Preservation Trust was awarded the lease.

In early October 1999, we stood in the west doorway and took stock – none of the joinery you see today was there then. It took six 10-tonne lorries to remove all the garbage, old bedsteads and so forth that had accumulated in the church.

We managed to raise almost half a million pounds towards the restoration from local people within a year. In addition English Heritage contributed £400,000, which enabled us with a bit of borrowing from the bank to undertake Phase 1 works of a £1m contract. But the real winner, the gift that made the whole thing possible, was the £2.452m from the Heritage Lottery Fund, and fundraising continued until it reached over £5m. Phases 2 and 3 major works contracts commenced in May 2007 and were completed in August 2009.

The main item of work, having lifted the floor to do the underpinning, was to put in a new steel floor structure; the old floor then went back on top of that. The third phase, run in parallel, entailed excavating underneath the floor to provide space for toilet blocks and six classrooms.

St Stephen's had been deconsecrated in 2002. The building re-opened for business in September 2009 with Hampstead Hill School moving in some of its pupils to occupy the lower ground floor during school hours, for

*Some of the accumulated rubbish in St Stephen's*
*Photo: St Stephen's Restoration and Preservation Trust*

which it pays the Trust a commercial rent.

Much of the stained glass had been stolen 30 years ago soon after the building was closed. What we had left is all Clayton and Bell – in the sanctuary it's early Clayton and Bell, whereas in the Lady Chapel it's late Clayton and Bell. To my mind that is the best Victorian stained glass one is going to see.

The mosaics survived. They were designed by Salviati of Venice but manufactured in the UK to his designs. They represent all the main religious symbols: on the left of the sanctuary is an Alpha and on the right an Omega.

We now have a licence to perform weddings and civil partnership ceremonies, and the building is used for concerts, theatre, corporate events, social events, and book launches.

*Michael Taylor is chairman of the*
*St Stephen's Restoration and Preservation Trust*

The Anglican church of St Stephen, early 1870s, *archive, hand coloured*
The church was designed by Samuel Saunders Teulon and is regarded as one of the finest late Gothic Revival buildings. At its peak, the church held up to 1,200 worshippers. Teulon considered it the best of the 114 churches he designed, calling it his "mighty church". Construction commenced in 1869, and it was consecrated four years later. The building is now Grade I-listed and is open for community use. It is again under serious threat, due to the Royal Free Hospital's project for its new Pears Building to be constructed adjacent to the green.

St Stephen's Interior in 2016

BELSIZE Remembered

# The Touching Story of Spencer House
## *Priscilla Sharp*

Numbers 9 and 11 Belsize Park Gardens were bought by Annie and Lucy Spencer in 1900 as a boarding establishment and became known as Spencer House.

In the 1920s Florence Richardson, who was the widow of Spencer Richardson, a nephew of Annie and Lucy, and her two children, Norman Spencer and Lucy Maud, went to live with "the Aunts". By the 1930s Spencer House had become the centre of local social life. Dances were held every Saturday evening in the drawing room of No.11. Evening dress was always worn and there was live music with the grand piano – which is still there – as the basis of the orchestra.

Then they acquired No.13 Belsize Park Gardens and decided to build a bridge between Nos.11 and 13 so as to have covered access between the houses. When this was complete, there had of course to be a Grand Opening. Red carpet was laid down on the pavement outside Spencer House and an important looking car was hired. This vehicle stopped alongside the red carpet and those well-known local dignitaries, the Duke and Duchess of Pork, stepped out to perform the ceremony. By this time quite a crowd had gathered to see what was going on and greeted the "Duke", a very small person and the "Duchess", a very tall, imposing-looking figure who had a suspiciously deep voice, with enthusiasm and cheers. The "Duchess" then very graciously accepted a beautiful bouquet which on closer inspection turned out to be skilfully made of vegetables.

In the 1930s many of these young people got married and gradually the residents became older as, indeed, did the Aunts. By the time World War II started Florence had taken over running the hotel as the Aunts had retired but still lived there. Florence was very short, with a wonderfully kind nature. She gave a home to a great many refugees and people who had nowhere else to live. Unfortunately they also had very little money and by the end of the war financial disaster was looming.

Norman, who had married Joan de Normanville Guy in 1936, reluctantly agreed to take over the running of Spencer House. Despite their misgivings they turned this ailing business around so that by the end of the 1950s Spencer House had once again become a successful hotel.

In 1961 they decided to sell. Hampstead Homesteads agreed to buy Nos.9 and 11 to provide accommodation for retired people who had lived most of their lives in Hampstead but could no longer live in their own homes. This was financed by Lieutenant-Colonel Ashley-Scarlet, Mayor of Hampstead, who raised £3,000 through his Mayoral Charity Appeal. With this sum, plus two low-interest loans from Hampstead Council, Hampstead Homesteads were able to purchase the leases of the two houses.

When this was publicised in the *Ham&High*, 100 applications were received. All the applicants were visited by the Hon Secretary, Mrs Laurie Randall, and the first residents were offered accommodation.

Mrs Randall carried on as Hon Secretary until Circle 33 took over the management of the House in 1988. Her commitment and devotion to the House and the support and interest of the committee fostered the happy, homely atmosphere which still permeates the House.

When Lieutenant-Colonel H Ashley-Scarlet died he left about £36,000 to Hampstead Homesteads.

**The founding committee members were:**
Lieutenant-Colonel H Ashley-Scarlet – Chairman
Mr Donald Frazer – Vice Chairman
Mr Stanley Duncan – Treasurer
Mrs Laurie Randall – Hon Secretary
Mrs Edna Lowther
Mrs Davis Buckley Sharp
Mrs Marrin Lowry
Mrs Donald Frazer
Mrs Stanley Duncan

IMPORTANT BUILDINGS

Spencer House in 2016

BELSIZE Remembered

# Vandervell's Garage Haverstock Hill

## Martin Humphery & Angela Vandervell Humphery

Following their service in WWI, brothers Frank and Percy Vandervell – Angela Vandervell's great uncles – acquired the property located between Belsize Avenue and Ornan Road on Haverstock Hill. This transaction included a large Victorian mansion called Belleview, complete with tennis courts, located on the northern side by Ornan Road. This house was to later become the offices and motor car showroom for a new business.

The two brothers put forward a plan in 1929 to develop the site into a "super garage". Inevitably, this proposal to build a filling station, a car laundry and motor showroom dominating most of the frontage between Ornan Road and Hampstead Town Hall met with considerable local opposition. The proposal had been reported in the *Hampstead and Highgate Express* in the 2 September edition of that year. The principal fear of local residents was that Belleview house was going to be demolished, but this was totally unfounded since it was to be retained and used as offices and the motor car showroom. But later, in about 1938, it was in fact pulled down and a new showroom built with a slender tower carrying the firm's name illuminated in neon. The brothers proceeded to construct a purpose-built garage adjoining the big house for a large petrol station and forecourt with direct access from Haverstock Hill.

During WWII Vandervell's Garage contributed to the war effort which included the waterproofing of army vehicles in 1944 in preparation for the D-Day landings.

My connection with the company began in 1954 after completing my National Service. Determined not to return to the law, which I had studied for several years after leaving school, I was most fortunate to be taken on in a junior role.

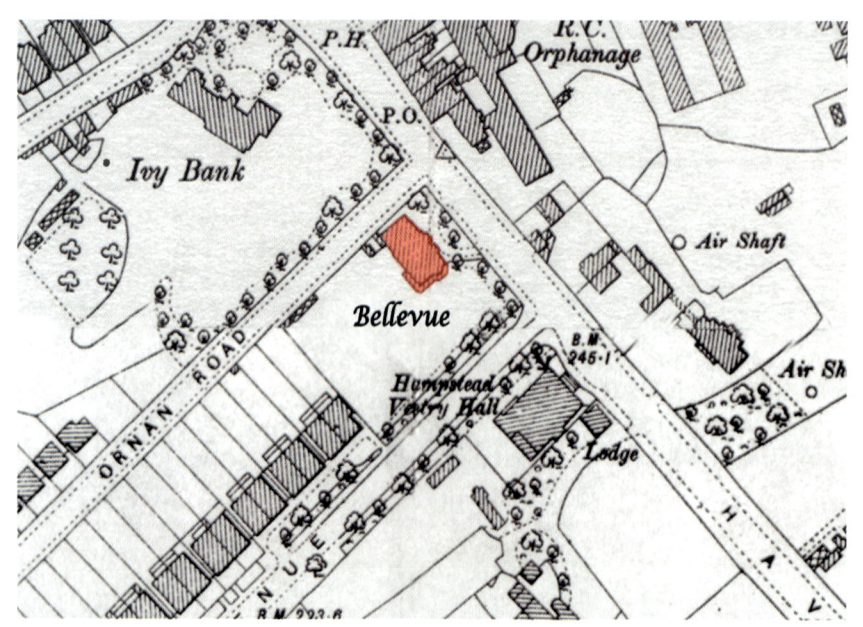

Belleview House and grounds on an 1896 map

*The Motor Trader and Review*

The Authoritative Journal of the Industry.
EVERY WEDNESDAY.

**PRESERVING THE AMENITIES IN HAMPSTEAD.**

MESSRS. PERCY AND FRANK VANDERVELL have now opened their garage and service station at 215, Haverstock Hill, Hampstead. The beautiful old house that stood on the property of two acres is being left as it was, and development of the site is proceeding steadily, so that it should be complete by the motor show. The brothers Vandervell will be pleased to see any old friends who call. The place itself is not without its instructional value as to what can be done with existing property without loss of efficiency and without spoiling the neighbourhood.

*The Motor Trader and Review,* July 1930

It was in this new job that I made the acquaintance of my wonderful future father-in-law who gave me a thorough grounding in the business that enabled me to enjoy a long career in the motor trade. In 1956 Angela and I were married.

Vandervell Bros Ltd was run as a franchise for the most popular marques of those days including Austin, Ford, Morris, Riley, and Vauxhall. The garage was a very successful company through to the early 1960s, as it was the only filling station on the left hand side of the busy northern route out of London, selling over a million gallons of fuel a year. In its heyday the premises were immaculately kept, with its attendants in smart white overalls. Then in 1964/65 it was bought by Guy Anthony "Tony" Vandervell, a cousin of Angela's father, who was a multi-millionaire, owner and CEO of Vandervell Products, the largest European manufacturer of shell bearings for motor engines, a racing financier, and founder of the Vanwall Formula One team. The Vanwall racing car won nine Grand Prix and the Constructors Championship in 1958. Tony was fortunate to have Stirling Moss in his team.

Tony Vandervell decided to sell up to a property developer in 1966. In turn it was acquired by the Trust House Forte group and converted into a hotel, retaining the filling station and forecourt. The hotel building has since changed ownership several times, but the filling station is still there (now run by BP) and is still doing good business. The site has pumped petrol continuously since the 1930s.

Vandervell Bros Ltd shortly after opening in 1930, *archive*

Stirling Moss in the Vanwall driving in the 1958 Dutch Grand Prix
*Photo from Brooks Summer Vintage catalogue, 1993*

Daffodils on Haverstock Hill, spring 2017

Crossing Glenilla Road

Meeting up in Belsize Village

'Make Tea, Not War' a Bansky-style stencil depicting Mrs Beechey, a retired shopkeeper who owned a hardware store in Regent's Park Road for 50 years

Belsize Lane, Belsize Village, 2012

BELSIZE Remembered

# Belsize Avenue's Green and Pleasant Verges
## *Judith Nasatyr*

My family moved into a house in Belsize Avenue in 1967 and I lived there for 45 years. At that time there were more bed sitters in the avenue than family homes. During the day our car was often the only one parked in the road.

No.30, on the corner with Glenilla Road, belonged to the Howard League for Penal Reform. It was thought that some boys who got into trouble with the police would benefit from living away from their home environment and the bad influences they encountered there. We never had any problems with them. The most troublesome neighbours were noisy coach parties of tourists who regularly woke everyone up coming home to a privately-owned tourist hostel. Luckily that didn't last very long.

Three new housing developments were built while we lived on the avenue: one privately developed block of flats, one council block and one block offering sheltered housing. The four houses on the site of the latter were in the process of being refurbished when one night, with a fearsome noise, they collapsed.

The grass verges and mature trees are the pride of the avenue. They were well tended in the early 1970s, regularly fed and weeded. The lawns were mowed weekly or fortnightly and were protected by metal chains fixed to concrete bollards.

There followed a period of neglect when broken posts were not replaced, chains were removed and weeds flourished. At its worst we mowed and tended our own patches of lawn and watched as builders working on house conversions stored building materials on the lawns leaving weedy or sandy patches when they moved on. There was even a short period when cars parked on the grass verges. Needless to say there were protracted negotiations between the Belsize Residents' Association and Camden Council.

These resulted in wooden posts and new chains being installed. Surprisingly, the other development that was to protect the grass verges was the advent of controlled parking.

'Thin Lizzie', the rock band that was formed in 1969, lived on Belsize Avenue with their women and children. When the group loaded up their transport vans with all their gear before leaving on tour I remember watching their families gather on the pavement to see them off.

Walking the dog on Belsize Avenue

IN AND AROUND THE VILLAGE

The grass verges of Belsize Avenue, spring, 2012

Belsize Avenue, 2013

# Living in Belsize Lane in the 1940s

## June Gibson Williams

Both my grandparents were employed by headmistress Miss Wright as live-in caretaker and cook at St Christopher's School, 32 Belsize Lane, with my mother as a general help. I was part of the family package!

St Christopher's was closed during WWII so it was in rather a bad state having been requisitioned for use as an ARP barracks for some years. My family had to prepare the school for the re-opening. Much elbow grease for cleaning and painting was expended. Miss Wright and her housekeeper Edith lived at No.20 Lyndhurst Gardens, as did her secretary Mrs Tuxford with her daughter Julie who was my age. Miss Wright was very well known in the area, often seen with her distinctive green cape as she cycled around Belsize.

Miss Wright extended the gym and obtained the lease of 20 Lyndhurst Gardens at the back of the property. This became the Junior School, and the wall between the two buildings was removed to create a single, large garden. Following the re-opening, the number of pupils soon increased. There were 120 two-course lunches to serve during term time, as well as catering for morning and afternoon breaks, all undertaken with the help of just two part-time scullery maids.

I attended Bartrams RC convent school (now the Rosary RC School) on Haverstock Hill as my family couldn't afford the fees at St Christopher's. Bartrams school was LCC funded so it was obliged to take children of any faith. The nuns were a well-known sight in Belsize Park, they used to wear the full fig – large metal crucifixes round their waists with their long black habits a-swirl. I remember there was a 'secret garden' behind Bartrams with a lovely little grotto to which pupils were occasionally taken for a visit. Later, the garden became the site of Bartrams hostel, and now Bartrams hostel itself stands there no more.

My first pet cat came from a neighbour in Lyndhurst Gardens who used to chat to me over the garden wall. I went round to the house to choose from the litter of kittens playing around a large cat basket in the kitchen. The huge, bright kitchen contained three or four maids bustling about, all dressed in starched white aprons and caps over blue uniform dresses. The dazzling scene has never left me.

There was always a biscuit or two for me when we visited the local grocers, including the two small J. Sainsbury shops on Haverstock Hill (so very different from today's Sainsbury's stores). Rationing, where applicable, was unkind but was probably good for our health! There was no refrigerator at St Christopher's, hence the need for frequent purchasing of perishables.

There was a water pit used for fire fighting during the war located on the corner of Belsize Avenue where the BP filling station and the Premier Inn stand today. The site was previously occupied by Vandervell's car dealership [p104]. The Odeon cinema on Haverstock Hill was permanently closed, so for us it was the Playhouse on South End Green, later the Classic cinema (now an M&S foodhall), or perhaps a walk to the Odeon at Swiss Cottage.

Often we would chat to the lamp lighter in Belsize Lane on his bicycle round at dusk. The horse-drawn milk cart came by in the mornings; grandfather always had a cuppa for the milkman and water for the horse – welcome refreshment for both. Frequent coal deliveries into the school cellar were vital to feed the pot-bellied stoves for winter heating of the classrooms. And during term time, a team of jolly hair-netted women in boiler suits came twice weekly with a lorry to collect the refuse (little packaging then!) including 'pigswill' bins full of scraps, kept separately.

St Stephen's was still a consecrated church in the 1950s – my grandmother's funeral service was held there in 1955. These were an idyllic few years for me, which I remember with great fondness.

I used to walk to my school on Haverstock Hill, leaving just before St Christopher's pupils began to arrive, and returned 'home' as most of them had left for the day. Even then children were warned never to speak to any strangers hanging about between the two schools. I particularly recall the sweet shop near Bartrams school offered many items off ration, at just a penny each – a very popular place with Bartrams' kids! And one day at assembly we were called in turn to each receive a shiny red apple from a food parcel sent from Canada. I don't think I had ever tasted a fresh apple before.

During the school holidays I accompanied grandfather on his errands, be it to pay rates at the Town Hall or to order school provisions. And I particularly remember the toy shop that I loved on Rosslyn Hill, which amazingly is still there. The shops on Belsize Lane, now known as the Village, were handy for immediate personal needs – perhaps a haircut at the barber's for grandfather, or perhaps 'Chicks' Own' or 'Tiny Tots' comics for me from the paper shop.

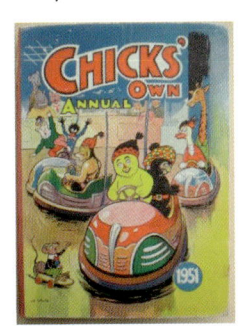

Belsize Lane and St Christopher's School in 2011

BELSIZE Remembered

# The Belsize Rubber Stamp

*Darel Seow*

I had the honour of creating a series of twenty rubber stamps, impressions of Camden, based on featured locations nominated by residents. These ranged from international and famous landmarks, such as the British Museum, to private ones such as a family home which housed three generations under one roof. Regardless of the location, each stamp represented a resident's personal connection to Camden and its various facets. The stamps are available for public use in libraries and are also displayed on the foyer walls of the new council building at No.5 Pancras Square.

There are two main aspects to the design of these stamps – the first being the outer, physical façade of the landmark which anyone would recognise at first glance. Delving deeper, the second feature would involve a distinctive view of the interior with which residents would be familiar. In the creation of these designs, I focused on the human angle of each location, illustrating how residents use and interact with these landmarks. Inspired by vintage travel posters, I employed simple graphic shapes to illustrate the buildings.

My trip to Belsize Village had caught my eye and thus formed the perfect view from which I could capture the essence of Belsize.

The triangular piazza is eye-catching, lined with attractive shops – each reaching a little higher than the one before, like steps. I could imagine residents, each with their unique tale waiting to be told, crossing paths as they traversed this picturesque space daily. I snapped a few quick photographs of this charming scene, for the stamp's design had already begun to take form in my head. A packed itinerary meant that I had to be on my way soon after. Despite my short visit, I know I'll definitely be back – perhaps to patronise the shops, partake in some gastronomical delights or just to pause on one of the benches and appreciate Belsize Park.

The Belsize rubber stamp *by Darel Seow*

IN AND AROUND THE VILLAGE

# Coal Hole Covers
## *David S Percy*

Belsize Village and Primrose Gardens are two locations around Belsize Park where one can still see a number of these surviving decorative pieces of street furniture in the form of cast iron coal hole covers. Typically, the coal hole hatch had a decorated iron circular cover set into the pavement that was unlatched from the inside. These are in fact apertures through which coal was tipped into the cellar below without the coalman needing to enter the property. The coal was then taken to fireplaces located in rooms throughout the house by scullery maids. Coal was widely used for domestic heating from the early 19th century until the middle of the 20th century.

Virtually all the covers had moulded patterns which were raised to help prevent pedestrians from slipping on them in the wet or during icy weather.

The covers themselves were surprisingly varied as each foundry had its own designs which in some cases included the company name.

As a child I remember seeing coal being brought down the street by horse-drawn cart, and watching the dusty coalman lugging his loaded coal sacks over the pavement on his back.

The coalman and his clothes from head to foot were nearly always black with coal dust which managed to get absolutely everywhere. He generally wore a leather hat with a large leather flap extending over his shoulders and down his back for protection against the heavy sacks of coal.

The modern circular Belsize Walk plaques set into the pavement along a suggested walk through Belsize echo these traditional coal hole covers, and the London plane tree design on the plates is based on an actual leaf found in Belsize Park.

Belsize coal hole cover

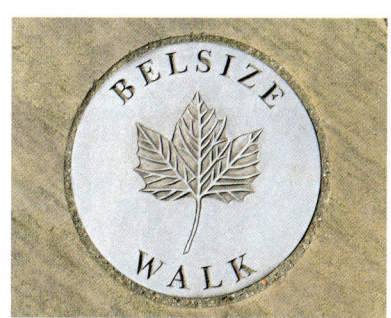

Belsize Walk plaque

Coalman and company cart out on delivery

BELSIZE Remembered

# The Witch's Cauldron in the Late 1950s

## Margaret Nolan

I started working at the Witch's Cauldron coffee bar in Belsize Village when I was 16, but had left before it became Conrad's Bistro in the 1960s. They had a very simple menu, items like steak and chips.

I remember they bought the steaks from the butcher's shop across the road (probably Coles, now the Belsize Village Deli), and all the food was purchased locally. Reg Conrad was the chef – a Cordon Bleu chef – and he taught me how to cook.

On Friday nights Reg would open up the cellar downstairs in the basement (which wasn't open during the week). I remember my mother thought the place was a den of vice, but it wasn't – well, maybe it was! I didn't pick up on that… It really was a cellar with little rooms off the main area. There were wax-encrusted candles in wine bottles as candle holders on all the tables, and they used to have wonderful folk music and blues musicians.

*The Witch's Cauldron, Belsize Village*

The Witch's Cauldron was a well-known basement club in the 1950s and 60s, a place where some people first heard the sounds of soul still enjoyed today (see also p150) –Ed.

# Waitressing at the Witch's Cauldron
## *Nicole Usigli*

When I first came up to London in 1961, I lived in Belsize Square. Most of the property in the area belonged to the Church Commission, but I had a private landlady. One day she sent the Irish housekeeper, Mary, to ask me to tidy up the piles of books, papers, etc., on the table in front of the window, as the mess could be seen from the street. The area was highly respectable, if rather run down.

I was waiting for an audition and had both time and need of money. Mary told me to ask if they needed waitresses at the Witch's Cauldron in Belsize Lane that we all went to. It belonged to Reg Conrad and later it became Conrad's Bistro. So I did occasional waitressing there and learned to use the coffee machine and make cappuccinos and sometimes had to scrub the huge saucepan in the tiny kitchen. Conrad was a lovely, burly man, who had a beautiful wife. One day the cashier did something wrong and got sacked on the spot and I was offered her job. The cashier got no tips, but it was the best job there because you sat comfortably on a high stool surveying the whole scene, and I got a free meal. I remember sometimes the female art students would get their long hair tangled with the spaghetti. The menu consisted of either spaghetti or risotto with the same sauce for half a crown, probably about £4 or £5 now.

Further along on the corner there was an antiques shop opposite the *Belsize Tavern*, the first pub I ever went to. At first the barman refused to serve me until my friends assured him I was old enough. Then I walked into the first loo I saw, and could not understand why my friends laughed so much when I came out. I'd used the men's loo. We all liked the friendly, warm and unpretentious atmosphere of the pub, and returned there often.

I left the area after a few months and came back, this time to Belsize Avenue, a few years later. I had a cat and took it to the lovely, kind, Mr Peters in Belsize Village. A big white cat who used to cross Belsize Park – there was not so much traffic in those days – but then he got run over. After that there was a letter in the *Ham&High* condemning the driver's carelessness!

In 1968, after years of waiting and requests, the 268 bus route started. It stopped just outside where I lived and it made life a lot easier when going uphill to Hampstead. I used to buy the paper from the news vendor outside Belsize Park tube station. I would ask for *The Times* and he would always reply "The Thames Gazette".

I now live in Aspern Grove, and it pleases me to see that although a lot of things have changed the basic character of the area has not altered that much.

BELSIZE Remembered

# Remembering Conrad's Bistro
## *Averil Nottage*

In the early 1970s I would go with a gang of friends to Conrad's Bistro, a cheap and cheerful French restaurant in the cellar where the Witch's Cauldron had been. The tables were in vaulted alcoves with gingham cloths and candles stuck in wax-encrusted wine bottles.

After a main course of something like coq au vin or boeuf bourginon I would always choose a négresse en chemise. This was a delicious combination of chestnut purée, cream and ice cream. At that time no one questioned its name.

We also went to Falafels, an Israeli restaurant on Haverstock Hill, a couple of doors down from the *Sir Richard Steele* pub. Looking back it doesn't seem very exciting, but Middle Eastern food was very unusual then. I don't think Conrad's Bistro survived much beyond the 1970s, but Falafels lasted for another 35 years.

A corner of Conrad's interior

Conrad's Bistro in the early 1970s

Conrad's Bistro, early 1980s

BELSIZE Remembered

# The Chateaubriand
## *Sergio Latorraca*

The Chateaubriand was a unique place, located next door to Conrad's Bistro and about half the customers were celebrities who lived locally. The speciality was of course the chateaubriand. We had a real charcoal grill which was our secret. The restaurant atmosphere was very cosy, with booths and small tables with candles – all very romantic. I knew quite a few people who were proposed to in one or other of our intimate booths.

When I first came to this country I didn't know many actors and celebrities, so for example, my customers would say to me, "Oh, that's Patrick Macnee who plays John Steed in *The Avengers*". In fact one of the locations they used was in Primrose Hill, so after filming they would come over to the Chateaubriand.

Lynsey de Paul was another regular, and she always introduced me to various celebrities who accompanied her as guests. One day she arrived, stood in the doorway and was obviously covering someone who was behind her. She said, "Sergio, I know that you don't know my guests, but I think you will know this one." She moved to one side, and behind her was Ringo Starr! – and of course I knew who he was!

Lynsey de Paul in 1974 *AVRO CC BY-SA*

David Suchet, the serious Shakespearean actor, used to live nearby in Fitzjohn's Avenue. I remember one day David came into the Chateaubriand with his wife and said, "I think I have something coming my way, a part in a new more commercial production," and then in 1989 he became Agatha Christie's Hercule Poirot, a role he played until 2013.

Frank Dickens, the cartoonist, best known for his strip *Bristow*, at about 11 in the evening would virtually crawl from the *Belsize Tavern*, crossing the road to the Chateaubriand. One night he said, "Let's celebrate! I would like a bottle of really cold Champagne and a very heavy kitchen knife." And as he was already rather tipsy, I was quite worried about giving him a knife from the kitchen, but Frank said, "Not to worry, not to worry." He was with a lady who replied, "Sergio, just let him do it!" So he took the bottle and struck it with the back of the knife, the blade hitting the lip broke the glass and separated the collar from the neck of the bottle, known as sabrage, and the cork flew out with the glass ring! After that almost every time he came in he would do this – all pretty dangerous!

The Chateaubriand clientele included actors, musicians and writers. The most recent one who has passed away was George Michael. On one occasion in the late 1980s, he was seated at the round table with five others. This time I recognised him, and as I knew my young girls were fans of George Michael I phoned home to tell them George was here. Of course they said, "Can we come over with our friends?"

So I went across to the table and said there are some admirers of yours that would like to come round to ask for your autograph. George's boyfriend immediately replied, "Yes, ask them to come over, Michael loves doing that – don't you darling?" And so the girls came over and he signed their autographs.

Belsize Park is very special to me. My first bedsitter was No.55 Belsize Park, near to Swiss Cottage. My second place was in the Village, next door to the Chateaubriand, at No.52 Belsize Lane, and now my own house is in Daleham Gardens. This means that I have moved around in an area of something like 500 yards!

The Chateaubriand, *by Sydney Arrobus*

Sergio Latorraca, Chateaubriand Manager, 1968-1995
*photo provided by S Latorraca*

Chateaubriand interior, *photo provided by S Latorraca*

119

BELSIZE Remembered

**CHATEAUBRIAND**
48 BELSIZE LANE, LONDON, NW3
Telephone: 01-435 4882

**Some of Sergio's customers at the Chateaubriand included:**

Larry Adler, musician
Michael Aspel, television presenter
Dan Aykroyd, actor and screenwriter
Stephanie Beacham, actor
Tom Conti, actor
Sue Cook, presenter and author
Frank Dickens, cartoonist
Fenella Fielding, actor
Marty Feldman, writer, comedian, and actor
Samantha Fox, songwriter, actress and former model
Bertold Goldschmidt, composer
Ian Holm, actor
John Hurt, actor
Derek Jacobi, actor
Jeremy Kemp, actor
Felicity Kendal, actor
Roy Kinnear, actor
Michael Kitchen, actor and television producer
Patrick Macnee, actor
George Michael, singer, songwriter, record producer and philanthropist
Patrick Newell, actor
Dennis Norden, writer and television presenter
Lynsey de Paul, singer-songwriter
Oliver Reed, actor
Michael Redman, technical theatre director
Norman Rossington, actor
Donald Sinden, actor
David Suchet, actor
Twiggy, model, actor and singer
Virginia Wade, tennis player
John Wood, actor

At the Chateaubriand, *photo provided by Patricia Tivy*

# A Knocking Shop in Daleham Mews

## Margaret Beccles

Years ago, from my window in No.21 Daleham Mews we used to observe some very strange comings and goings of the frequent visitors to No.10 Daleham Mews, which wasn't exactly opposite to us, but slightly to the right of our house. We tended to ignore all this action for a time, but then in the end we couldn't because there was such a lot of activity that we came to the inevitable conclusion that it was probably a rather upmarket knocking shop!

Years later when No.10 Daleham Mews was being remodelled this visiting card for Sylvia's Sortie Club was found under some floorboards.

Upper corner of Daleham Mews, 2011

BELSIZE Remembered

# From Delius to Breakdance
## *Selom Pomeyie*

My mother lived and worked in Nigeria before returning to the UK in the 1950s after her first marriage to an American Professor of Middle Eastern manuscripts had broken down. She shared a flat in Belsize Park Gardens with Shirley, a fellow trainee librarian, and went on to work at Keats Grove Library. When she finally settled with my father, she had decided that Belsize Park was the area where she wanted to start a family.

I, Selom, was born in 1976, two years after my brother, in the Royal Free Hospital and grew up with my mother, father and brother in a small top floor flat at No.44 Belsize Park Gardens, in one of the white double-fronted stucco houses. We later discovered that the composer Frederick Delius once lived in the house, which pleased my mother as they were both born in the same part of the UK (Yorkshire).

My mother became a link to everyone in the area. She would welcome new residents, smile at everyone, do good

*With mother and older brother, 44 Belsize Park Gardens*
*Photo provided by S Pomeyie*

deeds for people and talk to just about anybody, such as the students staying at the hostel three doors down. One of those students flew from Norway for a day to be at my mother's funeral. This warmth and friendliness was reciprocated by long-standing residents in the area, with smiles being a common way to give a passing greeting. A similar spirit may have existed in Belsize Park when Delius lived there, as conductor Thomas Beecham recalled that he was "warmly greeted by everyone".

My earliest memories largely revolve around the residents in the house, who mostly remained the same for the next 35 years. Eldred Evans and David Shalev, award-winning architects, lived in the flat below us with their daughter Teeny. They were occasionally driven mad by the noise two growing boys made through the creaky floorboards with no sound insulation. However, Eldred and David became a large part of why my mother never wanted to leave the flat, despite having to climb 77 stairs to the top.

David Hine lived in the basement flat and was my mother's carboot sale partner in crime. He was such a likeable man. He was also a huge fan of old Hollywood films and

*No.44 Belsize Park Gardens (blue plaque for Delius)*

used phrases like someone from *Biggles* with sayings such as "okay old chap", "marvellous old boy". As young children my brother and I found this hilarious. My mother had an empty space in her heart after David suddenly passed away whilst sitting on a bench opposite Belsize Park tube station.

Peta Button lived on the first floor for some time with TV producer Joe McGrath. They contributed to one of the most memorable moments of my young life when we were invited to come downstairs to a party to meet Eric Morecambe. I remember how funny he was, even to a seven-year-old boy. He immediately went into a routine about Atari computer consoles, which had all of the guests splitting their sides.

Peta and Joe's TV connections also resulted in my mum opening the door to Spike Milligan on more than one occasion. I suppose we took it for granted that these people were national celebrities. Famous faces are still regularly spotted in Belsize Park, perhaps drawn to the beauty of the place, but also as they are treated no differently to everybody else. Terry, Julian and Louise were the first local kids my brother and I played with. They lived in the cottage at the end of Glenilla Road.

Cottage on the corner of Glenilla Road, 2012

We used to play freely in the street and climb into the communal gardens of the mansion blocks on Belsize Grove. Many of the gardens back then had lower fences and were much easier to access. I'm not sure whether it's down to a change in times, a change in the area or both, but I don't see children exploring the area as we did back then.

As we grew older my brother and I started to make friends with other local young people. In my teenage years I became friendly with Jamie Beesley, Guy Higginson and Ben Dawson, all of whom remain some of my closest and oldest friends. Earlier, when I was nine, through my brother I met Tola Bashir, Fin Hardaker and his brother Sam, Olly Sylvester, Sam Hutchins. This group of friends used to congregate in the Belsize Village pizza shop. There was an arcade machine there which drew our attention. This was also the group of friends that went on to form a breakdance crew.

The 1980s saw the emergence of the breakdance phenomenon. There was already an older group of boys to be seen dancing in the Armoury on Pond Street called 'The Concrete Crew'. They took us under their wing, so we formed the 'Mini-Concrete Crew'. I was the younger (mascot like) member of the troupe. We would often congregate in the Village, lay a piece of lino on the pedestrianised triangle and start our moves. We drew interested glances from people using the local shops, but it was not until we were seen by a local hairdresser that we saw possibilities for the future.

Vaughn, the owner of the hairdresser's between Budgens and the Town Hall on Haverstock Hill, encouraged us to dance outside his shop to provide entertainment to passers-by (supposedly in the hope some might stop and get their hair cut). We learned that we could make a bit of pocket money by leaving a hat on the ground for tips, as we popped away and spun on our backs. *Break Dance the Movie* this wasn't, but it added character to an area that was comfortable with its identity as home for various demographics and cultures. One day Vaughn invited us to perform at a fashion show >

he was involved in. Needless to say this was the pinnacle of our short careers.

The Belsize Festival was a regular event in the 1980s where every local face was to be seen. I'm not sure why the festivals stopped, but during the time they were on it gave the area a real community spirit. Weeks before the festival friends would nonchalantly mention anything they had heard about that year's programme of events and entertainment. There were stalls selling food, bric-à-brac and homemade jewellery. Maypole dancing and live music was also a common feature. With all of the festivities going on it was also a chance to do a bit of breakdancing.

In my teenage years I spent most Fridays playing football on the old astro pitch at *the Winch*, at the end of Fellows Road. Everybody loved *the Winch* – it was one of the few places in the area that allowed young people to let off steam, either in the community centre or on the hard, sandy Astro-Turf. Mick McDonnell (brother of the boxer Jim) used to run the sessions. Everyone would pay their £1.50 sub for the session, even though for most that was their weekend pocket money. Occasionally someone would turn up without any money but Mick would airily say pay it next week.

Mick was there like clockwork, every Friday. The only Friday when the session didn't fully run was the night of the famous Arsenal vs Liverpool game in 1989. Mick cut the session short so he could watch the game. Most of us were happy as we were Arsenal fans!

The physical landscape has changed over the last 30 years with the felling of some trees and the arrival of some large chain coffee shops and mini supermarkets. However, Belsize Village, thanks to the support of the locals, has many of the same shops, Oddbins [this was written in 2013], the Late Late Store, Late Nite Extra [alas no longer] the Indian restaurant and the laundrette. A greater change has come in the feel of the community, as some of the previous residents have given way to bankers and city workers, with a higher turnover of residents. Nevertheless, for me Belsize will always be a place where people can live harmoniously and get creative inspiration from its tranquillity. According to Delius, this is the only true happiness in life.

Belsize Village, including Oddbins (far corner) and Late Nite Extra (on the right), 2011

# Lambolle Place
## Robert Labi

Lambolle Place was for years not just a place for car maintenance and repairs but also light industry. I remember a strike at a small metal and plastic working factory there in the very early 1960s. For a time the former Marchi-Zeller bakery, which then was based in Mornington Crescent, kept their delivery lorries in a large garage which, sometime later, was taken over by the SpringHealth leisure club as they expanded the former Hampstead Squash and Rugby Fives premises at No.81 Belsize Park Gardens.

Prior to this, these premises had been occupied by the Bhagwan Shree Rajneesh's Orange People movement. They were very welcoming to people who came in (I seem to remember them having open disco nights) and soon were locally known for their very friendly recruitment methods.

Lambolle Place, 2017

BELSIZE Remembered

# Letter from America

## James C Cox Jr

During the summer of 1982, while serving aboard the aircraft carrier USS *America* (CV 66) I received a call from Naval Intelligence in Washington, telling me the navy had decided to send me to London later that year. I hemmed and hawed awhile, finally admitting I was getting pretty serious about a girl and that going overseas really did not fit my plans. I was told, too bad, that I could go to London accompanied (married) or unaccompanied (single), but I was going! I called my sweetie up, telling her about my pending orders to London. I told her I could go in one of two ways. After explaining what accompanied and unaccompanied meant, she said, "of course, accompanied", and that was that. We were married in early October, and flew to London a couple of weeks later.

After several nights in a hotel, we ended up in Belsize Village, where we were to remain until the summer of 1985.

So here we were, new wife, new job (first shore duty), new country, and all of that!

Our address was No. 4 Copperbeech Close, a tiny modern group of houses off Akenside Road. We loved it. Our neighbour and landlord, Neville, was the best. He was a very liberal man who loved discussing world issues with me, a United States Naval Officer, whom (I suppose) he considered a real conservative. We spent many hours talking, arguing, and mostly laughing. Couldn't have been better.

When I think of our life in London, my first thoughts turn to the Village Curry Centre. We discovered Indian food in London, and we ate at the Curry Centre, oh, probably five nights a week. We both worked late and we would just take the short walk down there and eat. I remember the first time we did take-out! Hey…some of those colours that we had not noticed in the restaurant were pretty intense under the bright lights of our dining room. I have come to realize since that the Curry Men Cricket team was organizing at the same time and same place. I expect we shared some dining with them, though

Springtime, Copperbeech Close

we never connected.

Next I remember, so well, Oddbins. I was crushed when I read it had been sold. I cannot believe how much wine we bought there. In London I switched from reds to whites and have never looked back. We also developed a fine taste for DP. Wow! How many bottles of that walked up the hill to our house with me.

Then the Village butcher. He was across the little square from Oddbins, not quite as far as the pub. At the time, the television show *Dallas* was rather popular and he lapsed into his Dallas voice every time we came in. Our North Carolina, southern accents reminded him of Dallas, I guess. Anyway, he was great. We bought ducks, rabbits, and all kinds of game from him, as well as lots of meat, that he would gladly cut "American style" for us.

One day the shop was closed. I asked around and it turned out he had won the pools. The story was that he closed in the early morning, paid off his employees mid-morning, and had left by early afternoon. When asked where he was going, he said "I am going fishing." We missed him, but were happy for his good fortune.

We got our first Christmas tree together at Crescent Fruiterers on the corner, just across the street from Oddbins. It was a little scrawny, but hey, first Christmas together and all that mess. I had the 11:00pm to 8:00am duty on Christmas eve at the US Navy Headquarters, so I had to make the trek to the tube station at about 10:30pm. Still remember hearing Christmas carols being sung while I made my walk.

We did not spend much time in the pub, I have some breathing problems and can't deal with smoke very well, but it seemed like a cool place. We ate at a number of small restaurants in the Village, I can't remember their names, but without children and a small kitchen, we were certainly diners out. One I especially liked was a couple of doors down from the greengrocer.

We used to love walking around the neighbourhood, looking at the homes and gardens, walking over to the Heath, or up and down the streets up in Hampstead. We had a small American car that we took over. Used to park it between two Rolls Royces, what a hoot! I wish I had a picture of that.

I have been stationed all over the world, but without exception, if given an opportunity to return to one duty station, it would be to Belsize Village. We loved it.

Oddbins interior in 2011, virtually as it was originally – at the time the oldest shop in the Oddbins group

BELSIZE Remembered

# Life in Hostels
## *Elaine Joan Spencer*

In 1966 my government department arranged accommodation for me with the London Hostels Association. I moved to No.30 Belsize Park Gardens although the communal areas and meals were served at Nos.38 and 40. The houses had large bay windows at the front on the basement and ground floors. The steps up to our big wooden front door, with two round arched glass panels were tiled in a black and white diamond pattern. In the hallway was the residents' telephone. In 1967 our phone number was 'Primrose Next Year'.

Steps to No. 30 Belsize Park Gardens

There were up to six per bedroom with a bathroom attached, but the toilet was in the corridor. Many women brought soft toys to personalise their space. My grandmother made me a 'gonk', like Humpty Dumpty, quite popular at the time. Civil Servants under 18 were allowed weekly day-release classes for academic subjects. I did my homework in the "quiet lounge". We had a laundry room, but I also used the laundrette on the corner opposite Belsize Park tube station.

Our hostel warden closed the television lounge at a set time – even for the first Moon landing, so we missed the live broadcast. I watched it in the window of a television shop the following lunchtime. In the hostel basement there was a table tennis room in which the hostel committee organised a weekly social evening.

Meals were provided. We bought extras from a 'mini market' on the corner of Belsize Terrace and Belsize Avenue, a delicatessen in Belsize Park run by an Austrian couple, and cakes from Grodzinski's opposite the tube station, next to Stanfield's Opticians.

Benos café adjacent to the Odeon, *archive*

Other haunts were Benos café (which shared a kitchen with the Capri restaurant next door) by the Odeon cinema, the Swiss Grill opposite (there was another branch opposite Finchley Road station) and *The George* on the corner of Rowland Hill Street. Nearby there was a sign outside saying 'Loyal to the British Flag'.

*The George,* Haverstock Hill c.1966 *photo provided by E Spencer*

Some residents supplemented their salaries with evening work, ushering at the Odeon on Haverstock Hill, which gave staff complimentary tickets to pass on. So we regularly went to the cinema.

At weekends we often walked to Hampstead Heath via Pond Street. We peered through the fence at stray kittens living on the site that later became the Royal Free Hospital. Once we saw an old lady feeding them.

On the way to the station, I remember slipping about on ice while walking past the house with the blue plaque in Howitt Road where Ramsay Macdonald lived. Friday was *Ham&High* day. The paper was sold outside the station, where a blind man played an accordion. Friday evenings saw us at The Tinkers Folk Club sitting on the stove (for a good view), upstairs at *The Three Horseshoes*, Hampstead; latterly in theatre seats at the Country Club, Haverstock Hill when The Tinkers moved there. They were Irish: Gerry Fox, Maureen and Mick. Years later, after looking round a property in Harrow, my brother asked me if I recognised the vendor's husband. It was Gerry Fox. I bought the flat.

I know of three marriages between people who met at the hostel: three Irishwomen, two Scotsmen and a Yugoslav (one of several the hostel employed). He married at St Peter's, Belsize Square. My boyfriend and I went to the Town Hall on Haverstock Hill one Saturday morning to ask if we could book there to get married. We were told to come back on a weekday but we never did! My boyfriend left afterwards to join the RAF. I once saw the comedian Marty Feldman walking past there. I attended one wedding at the Town Hall. There I also attended my first hustings meeting, having become eligible to vote between 18 and 21 when the law changed. The third couple I met again, years later, coincidentally in Harrow, where they too had moved.

In the 1970s I moved to Netherlands House, 3 Nutley Terrace; then to Ames House Hostel, 26 Netherhall Gardens. Netherlands House had a communal self-catering kitchen, but provided breakfast which included Dutch cheese. An International club used a room on the ground floor. At a hall in Nutley Terrace I once heard Margaret Thatcher, then Education Minister, speak in support of a local candidate.

Ames House Hostel in Netherhall Gardens was originally for seamstresses. In the >

No.3 Nutley Terrace, 2016

1970s occupations included studying at St Godric's Secretarial College, and occupational therapy in Eton Avenue.

Breakfast was provided. There was a refrigerator and bathroom on each landing. Each bedroom (for up to three) had a kitchenette (which could be closed off with a Venetian blind) comprising Baby Belling cooker, sink, draining board and cupboard. I bought food from a shop next to Finchley Road station.

We were allowed to entertain visitors. When it was visitor leaving time, we decanted our party to the *Bierkeller* or the Purple Pussy Cat discotheque off Finchley Road. But by then the party atmosphere had gone.

Outings included walking the Warden's Labrador on Hampstead Heath; the Classic cinema on South End Green; and visiting cafés: Habana, Carmel, Pisces, Fleet Road chip shop and *The Moon and Sixpence* on a steep bank in College Crescent. Once, returning from Richmond Ice Rink to Finchley Road and Frognal station, all the stations were in darkness: there was a partial power cut.

My sister Marion lived at Ames House for a while. Our grandmother came to stay one weekend. As well as showing her the Hampstead sights, we visited the show flat in Imperial Towers, which was being built opposite the hostel on the corner of Netherhall Way.

Marion and I were on the Netherlands House International Club Committee. My brief was theatre visits. We had ballroom dancing lessons at the club, but were both slow learners.

Marion ran a Brownie Pack at Holy Trinity Church opposite Finchley Road station. She remembers (when the church was closed) attending service in a shop on Finchley Road; the confined space created a friendly atmosphere as people sat close together. She also remembers regularly walking to a station further away to save money. Probably there was a fare stage south of Finchley Road station.

Shortly before I left Ames House to work abroad, I had my eyelashes dyed black and eyebrows plucked at Madame Borel's in Frogmore Parade, Finchley Road.

Ames House, Netherhall Gardens in 2016

IN AND AROUND THE VILLAGE

# Closing off Rat Runs
## *Mayer Hillman*

We had been living in our house on Netherhall Gardens for over 37 years. For about half of that time our life was blighted by the fact that part of the road had become a commuter rat run – used by motorists diverting from the Finchley Road through Netherhall Way and across to Fitzjohn's Avenue.

We were in the process of asking Camden Council to close off Netherhall Way, converting it into a cul-de-sac, when we discovered that a similar attempt was being made to close off the top of Belsize Terrace from Belsize Lane, bringing to an end another commuter rat run, this one through Belsize Village. We therefore joined forces on that idea and both proposals were eventually successful.

The closures have brought phenomenal benefits for both areas.

Belsize Village before closure of Belsize Terrace, c.1980, *archive*

Belsize Village spring 2011

BELSIZE Remembered

# Lifelong Romance Began in Belsize Park Gardens

*Michael Roberts*

It was early April 1969. I stepped out of a London black cab late on a Sunday night and was impressed by the large white building before me. I had by then travelled some 200 miles by fruit lorry from Torquay to Covent Garden and from there by taxi. This was my first visit to London. No.40 Belsize Park Gardens was to be my first London address and it looked very impressive. A discreet plaque on the wall confirmed it was a LHA (London Hostels Association) building set up to provide affordable accommodation for young civil servants coming to London from the provinces.

That main building housed the office and communal rooms; the adjoining No.38 provided the male bedrooms whilst the female bedrooms were in a separate building further up the road (No.32, if memory serves me right). The hostel provided a real community and friendship. I enjoyed playing football for the hostel football team in Primrose Hill on Sunday mornings.

I had come to London as a 17-year-old to start a career in the Post Office and began work in Swiss Cottage Post Office (18 Harben Parade Finchley Road), sadly no more. That summer a young girl approached my counter and asked for a stamp for a letter to Spain. She returned on subsequent days, always buying one 9d stamp (despite having to queue) and always had a lovely smile. After some time I plucked up courage to ask the young lady out for coffee. The combination of her limited English as a Spanish lady along with my attempts to keep the offer discreet (through the bandit screen) meant that the offer was not fully understood! However, she decided that whether I was asking if she liked coffee (which she did) or if I was asking her out, she would say yes to both questions and would suggest a time later.

Our early dates led to a growing love that had to survive Maria's return to Spain and a separation. In the meantime the postal service played a major role in our growing love. There was a slight interruption when the British Postal Service went on strike for seven weeks from 20 January 1971. When we went back to work in March we had to tackle the new decimal currency that had been introduced on the 15th of February.

While we were on strike I was able to find work in Salmon Florist (next to Belsize Park tube, another casualty of the times) and also in the Odeon cinema on Haverstock Hill (now in part a supermarket). Occasionally I supplemented my income by providing holiday cover at Belsize Village Post Office (also vanished) besides pulling pints in the evening at *The Haverstock Arms*, then run by the delightful Bunny and Pat. I remember serving by candlelight during power cuts!

Maria returned from Spain as an au pair with a family in St John's Wood and became my wife on 1 July 1972. We married, both aged 20, at St Thomas More Catholic Church on Maresfield Gardens. The photograph shows us leaving the church to go to the reception at *The Haverstock Arms* (South Hampstead High School in the background of the photograph is still there, but completely rebuilt.) Bunny gave us the reception room in *The Haverstock Arms* as a wedding present. *The Haverstock Arms* is no more and the building has become a boutique hotel [p155]. The family Maria worked for provided us with our first married home, a bedsitter in Carlingford Road.

We left London in order to buy our own family home and have been blessed with two children and three grandchildren. Back in the church for our 40th wedding anniversary, the priest gave us a special blessing and said he hoped we would return for our 50th. We have been back to Belsize Park several times since, taking many happy trips down memory lane. It feels like going home for both of us!

IN AND AROUND THE VILLAGE

Maria and Michael on 1 July 1972
*photo provided by M Roberts*

South Hampstead High School for Girls shortly after it was opened by Princess Louise in 1882 – now rebuilt, *archive*

BELSIZE Remembered

# Growing up in Manor Mansions

## David S Percy

Manor Mansions is located at the junction of Belsize Grove and Belsize Park Gardens and still looks virtually the same as when it was my home as a young boy in the 1940s.

It was among the first purpose-built apartment blocks to be constructed in London. Built in 1884 in red brick with stucco banding and detailing, the block is very different from and contrasts with the large stucco villa that was pulled down to make way for this replacement.

Our family lived on the ground floor, in flat 12 on the corner. A regular daily event was the arrival of a horse-drawn milk cart belonging to one of the dairies that used to stop just outside the block in Belsize Grove. I remember looking forward to helping the milkman offer up the nosebag to feed his horse just before he set off on his rounds of the flats.

After the war there were very few motorcars, if any, parked in the roads around Belsize. People often ask what the area was like in those days, and the clear, wide streets free of parked cars is probably the most visible difference that comes to mind. Of course this minimal car ownership meant that virtually all children had to walk to school. Mine was St Christopher's in Belsize Lane [p110], a very pleasant walk indeed. It was then, and still is, a girl's school but for a while after the war they took in boys as well.

Manor Mansions (on the right) at the junction of Belsize Park Gardens and Belsize Grove, c.1890, *archive*

IN AND AROUND THE VILLAGE

Belsize Grove from Belsize Park Gardens, c.1906, *archive*

Typical 1940s street scene, Belsize Avenue virtually free of parked cars, *archive*

# Happy Days in Primrose Gardens
## Deepa Gulhane

My mother came to London from a small village in India in 1952; my father arrived from another Indian village in 1947. My father's older sister and her husband – the first of our family to come to England – settled down in a property at the junction of Rosslyn Hill and Pond Street where they opened a boarding house for students from Asia. Later in the 1960s they started a Hindu temple. My uncle used to make and sell incense to sell from stalls in Petticoat Lane before the war, and in the Portobello Road in the late 1960s.

My mother's sister, assisted by my mother, also ran a boarding house for overseas students on Parliament Hill Road. My parents then married and moved into No. 36 Primrose Gardens in 1959.

I remember my mother mentioning that she paid something like £3,000 for the entire house. The house was full of sitting tenants. My parents had a struggle to keep the house as my mother worked in a sweet factory in Camden Town and earned very little money. The factory owners liked her as she didn't eat any of the sweets from the production line, unlike the others who seemed to be munching away all day long! The reason my mother didn't eat them was because she wasn't used to English sweets.

One day Mother noticed that the cellar doors in the basement of the house were often partly open, and she couldn't understand why, as no one from the household ever went into the cellar. One day she realised that a tramp was sheltering there every night. Apparently he was just down on his luck and was not a threat, so she gave him food and odd jobs around the house and let him sleep in the bath(!) for which he was very grateful. I remember him as the most decent, kind man I have ever met.

I don't recall my father ever going out to work, he probably stayed at home as we used to take in tenants. When I was

No.36 Primrose Gardens, 2016

My parents at No.36 Primrose Gardens, *photo provided by D Gulhane*

11 my father died. Mother still rented out rooms for income but started renting only to girls and running an informal B&B. Most girls were relatively low-paid workers such as waitresses. The breakfast provided was always excellent. Mother used to drive her small two-door Fiat to a farm in Totteridge and buy freshly laid free-range eggs.

In my early teens a French onion seller would come round on his bicycle selling his onions, they were always very tasty and reasonably priced. Then when I was about 13, we had a street party on Primrose Gardens to celebrate the Queen's Silver Jubilee. It was a really lovely sunny day, the road was closed off and all the tables were filled with party food. Happy days.

When I first started work at the age of 16, only a handful of people got on and off the Underground train at Belsize Park station, but these days almost an entire carriage seems to get off at Belsize Park!

I still live at the same address and have carried on the family business of running a B&B but have now decided to retire. Even after more than 30 years some of the girls who used to live in the house knock on the door, revisiting their youth. Sometimes I even recognise them.

In my younger days we weren't allowed to use the green in the island area of Primrose Gardens, but now it is wonderful to see young children playing there.

The green, Primrose Gardens in 2016

BELSIZE Remembered

# Early Years in Tudor Close
## *Mona Priwin Wynn Bradley*

All the photographs from my childhood show how happy I was to be in London. But something was to be the most terrifying thing I could remember, worse than the nightly vision of the Blitz would be, more frightening than the memories of a four-year-old girl's escape in 1936 from war-threatened Europe to the haven of Belsize Park had been. The dreadful wailing came ever closer, and a giant figure swayed ominously as it passed the corner just down from No.36 Tudor Close where I was standing, rigid with fear, as Mickey Mouse made his way down Glenloch Road, for some incomprehensible reason screeching on the bagpipes. I'm not sure whether I had ever been to the Odeon on Haverstock Hill, but if I had ever seen the cartoon character on the screen, it had not prepared me for this 20-foot effigy in glaring, clashing colours!

Other disturbing characters roamed the area too, who likewise turned out to be harmless enough: like the man with the glass eye – the father of a Christian Community priest whom I later knew and worked with over many years – though the site at 32 Glenilla Road was still a tennis court, and the Church I would come to love for so long was only a presence waiting in the wings.

I remember one very hot summer and a welcome dripping tap near the private garages of Tudor Close which was my best toy, at least until a boy called Brian Burtish turned up who shared his child-sized car with me. (Where are you now, Brian?) Later we played together through the long nights in our curtained-off cubicle at the back of the Tudor Close air raid shelter. On those occasions I pretended to be asleep, just to have the luxury of being carried there by my father on his strong shoulders; but I looked up fearlessly at the spectacular display of moving searchlights and explo-

Mona Priwin In Tudor Close, 1936
*photo provided by M Priwin*

sions of light in the sky.

More humdrum early memories include shopping on Haverstock Hill at J. Sainsbury, still the local grocer's rather than a supermarket. In this my fourth capital city I finally learned about shopping. It was such fun seeing the butter patted together with wooden paddles and wrapped in paper on demand. Kirry's was also a most popular delicatessen, which went on into the 1960s. It had barrels of pickled and salted herrings, and gherkins. I enjoyed that shop, perhaps because it reminded me of my previous homes. I recall too the fascination of travelling by tube from Belsize Park to Camden Town, my eyes fixed on the flickering red cable which ran along the tunnel just outside the window. My first experience of nature came with visits to Hampstead Heath and Golders Hill Park, where once a congregation of birds jostled for bread from someone on a bench, until our excited

Tudor Close, 2012

arrival frightened them away. I was distraught – but the stranger very kindly understood my distress and even more wonderfully showed me a nest in a hollow at the very base of a tree trunk, where I could look right in.

Then one day everything changed. My mother was surprised to discover that in England children had to go to school much earlier than on the continent. (My father was busy with his own life – he was then H W Priwin who wrote *Inspector Hornleigh Investigates*. Later he became John P Wynn who wrote *Brain of Britain* for the BBC.) So off I went. Kingsley School in Belsize Park offered some bewildering activities. 'Do you know the Muffin-man?' – actually, I didn't: what is a muffin anyway? – and still more why do you have to swing your arms stiffly up and down in front as you say it over and over again? I know now what muffins are, but the arm-movements remain baffling to me. Better than that, though, I played in a band. A percussion band. I was given two metal rods, one shaped into a triangle, the other short and straight, and told to join in. This was strange too but I quickly got the hang of it. However, as for learning my tables – I cunningly managed to avoid doing so until I was of an age when everyone assumed I must know them and gave up trying to teach me, to my permanent regret.

Most bewildering of all was the wholesale evacuation of the School in 1939 as the war drew ever closer. We left one morning in late August at seven in the morning, not exactly a ragged bunch of evacuees but well-behaved and in school uniform (with gas masks at the ready) to go first of all to South Hampstead railway station and from there – we knew not where. (To my delight ever after, we were sent to Tintagel!)

The School never returned. And there my connection with Belsize also came to an unexpected end – until destiny took a further turn and around 1951 brought me to the Christian Community, whose Church now stood at No.32 Glenilla Road [p94]. Its consecration had taken place in 1948, and from that time onward it was to be central in my life. The secretarial skills I had acquired were gladly put at the disposal of the movement, which had made that church its headquarters, so I was 'home' again – but now living in a series of more or less unsatisfactory bedsitters. After a spell in Primrose Hill, I had looked around in Belsize Park Gardens, then prime bedsit territory. One room had about ten worn-out carpets, each piled upon the other (the lifetime's collection of the landlady).

Further spells in flats followed, owned sometimes by families in considerable turmoil. These restless situations seemed all too common, and I was grateful finally to be given shelter by members of the Christian Community who lived in Howitt Road. This became my real home until I got married and left London to go and live in Oxford. For many years we continued Christian Community activities in our North Oxford house, and often thought of it as 'Glenilla Road-on-Thames'.

BELSIZE Remembered

# Belsize Village

*Jim Bowen*

I have lived in and around Belsize since I came out of university in the early 1960s. After qualifying as a pharmacist, I worked in various parts of London and decided that Hampstead/Belsize Park was to be the place where I'd like to settle down. I came from a Welsh village into an English village.

I purchased a pharmacy in Belsize Village, the only one there. Living above the shop, I remember coming down one Friday, and we hadn't taken any money by midday – not a penny had gone into the till. This was despite the fact that we had been doing extraordinarily well since we opened.

Then a friend of mine came in wearing a bowler hat. I told him, "I think I am going to go bankrupt if this goes on, as I haven't taken anything all morning."

He said, "Don't you realise you are in a Jewish area here, and it's a Jewish holiday – and nobody comes out until sunset."

"Thank God for that!" I replied.

Essentially it was quite a vibrant little village, it had everything one would have wanted. Later, in 1980, the Church Commissioners who owned the freeholds sold swathes of Belsize property to incumbent leaseholders: houses, flats and shops. I was lucky enough to be able to purchase a large portion of the Village, although it was rather run down at the time. Now over the years the Village has become very much more attractive and the shops have been spruced up with many attractive colour schemes.

Early morning in the Village, 2012

Belsize Terrace, c.1900, *archive*

Belsize Terrace, now part of Belsize Village, 2012

BELSIZE Remembered

# War Correspondent Finds Peace

*Oggy Boytchev*

When I was growing up behind the Iron Curtain in the Bulgarian capital, Sofia, in the shadow of the biggest Sephardic synagogue in Europe, I never thought that one day I would make my home in the vicinity of another synagogue, this time in north London, in the heart of Belsize Square.

From my childhood bedroom window on the third floor of a small apartment block, I stared for days on end, as I was doing my homework, at two stars not far away – the five-pointed star over the Communist Party Central Committee and the golden hexagram over the large dark grey dome of the synagogue. The Red Star, symbol of the Communist domination over the city, has long gone. The golden hexagram is still there.

I moved to London in the mid-1980s just before the fall of the Iron Curtain. The collapse of Communism in Eastern Europe was as spectacular as it was unexpected, even for politically active people like me. I claimed political asylum here at a time when we East Europeans were few and far between. Unlike the throngs of Bulgarian builders and cleaners who live in Britain today, the only Bulgarian most British people were aware of at the time was the writer Georgi Markov, killed by a poison-tipped umbrella on Waterloo Bridge in 1978. It was at the height of the Cold War and people's imagination was gripped by the real-life spy thriller events surrounding Markov's death. A micro-engineered pellet containing the deadly poison ricin was fired from an umbrella tip into his leg while he was waiting for a bus.

Four days later he died in hospital despite valiant efforts by British doctors to save his life. As with the poisoning of Alexander Litvinenko in London in 2006, the KGB and the Bulgarian secret service, KDS, were blamed for Markov's murder. A long-drawn-out investigation failed to establish conclusively who did it. The case still remains unresolved. But the phrase 'Bulgarian Umbrella' entered the everyday lexicon.

Eight years after his murder, I sat at Markov's desk in the Bulgarian Section of the BBC World Service at the start of my long, exciting career as a journalist.

My work for the BBC took me to many countries around the world where I covered war, civil conflict and assassinations, natural disasters, electoral triumphs and defeats. I saw death and destruction on an unimaginable scale. I met presidents and kings, warlords and freedom fighters. But I always came back to London as my home.

In the first years after my arrival in Britain, I found myself without a home, so for a while I crashed out on a friend's couch in Hillfield Court, the famous Art Deco mansion block off Belsize Avenue. This was when my love affair with Belsize Park began.

At the time it was rather run down. The atmosphere was bohemian – squatters lived in semi-derelict houses on Haverstock Hill. I made friends with some of them – impoverished artists, alternative types and asylum seekers of various nationalities.

It was the time of the first Gulf War (1990-91). Over cheap drinks, huddled around electric heaters we debated world events, the rights and wrongs of politics and war. When I wasn't with them, I went out to the West End almost every night. I was lucky then to meet my life-long partner, Julian.

After brief spells in East London and Highgate, I came back to Belsize Park, where I made my home.

Belsize saved my sanity. After some gruesome experiences in far-flung parts of the world I came to Belsize as a haven of peace and quiet. In 2003, during the second Gulf War, I was in charge of the BBC field operation in Northern Iraq. Two of my team lost their lives in the line of duty – a

Autumn on Hampstead Heath

cameraman died in a landmine explosion outside the city of Suleymania, and a local Kurdish translator was killed during the so-called 'friendly fire' incident when our convoy was bombed by a US fighter jet. One of my producers lost his leg in the same landmine blast. The team spent 72 days marooned in the north because all the surrounding countries had closed their borders – Turkey, Syria, Iran. The only way out was through Baghdad. It was a test of mental and physical endurance.

When I finally managed to make it to London, I was totally exhausted. A mental and physical wreck, I refused the offer of psychotherapy to combat the trauma sustained during my assignment. Living in the calm surroundings of Belsize Park helped me deal with it.

Day after day, waking up here I was confused about where I was. Was I still in Iraq? What story was I doing? Where was the rest of the team? But the dawn chorus in the surrounding gardens and the peaceful atmosphere restored my health.

After a stint in Baghdad, Kabul or Gaza, or after an undercover mission in Zimbabwe, my adrenalin levels were so high that waking up in the morning I was expecting to hear gunfire or the proverbial 'knock on the door'.

But riding my mountain bike on the Heath, in good weather or bad, in rain or sun, was the best therapy I could get. I still have an established cycling route – along Belsize Grove into Downside Crescent, turning left into Lawn Road and then onto Fleet Road towards South End Green, where I join the Heath.

Over the years, travelling to the most hostile places on earth as John Simpson's producer, Belsize kept me calm. Here, I wrote my book *Simpson & I: Between Two Worlds* documenting some of the most memorable stories ever to appear on BBC News.

Belsize Park feels like the countryside and yet it's so central. It's vibrant, cosmopolitan and liberal, like Greenwich Village in Manhattan. The bookshops, the pubs, the restaurants – they all have this idiosyncratic Belsize feel. But I think it's the residents that make Belsize so special.

It's a long way from downtown Sofia where I grew up. People ask me if I ever feel nostalgic about Bulgaria. "Only about food" I answer. And yes, if I feel nostalgic I could get a taste of Bulgarian cuisine at the Turkish restaurant on Belsize Lane [alas, there no more –Ed.], which serves Balkan food. But there's one thing I can't get in Belsize – no one makes chicken soup as my mum did.

BELSIZE Remembered

# Belsize Park in the 1960s and 70s

*Anthony Wills*

I first came to Belsize in 1968 when I shared a damp basement flat directly opposite the *Sir Richard Steele* pub. We would buy our drinks in the public bar and then move into the saloon bar to ogle the girls! I think that just before decimalisation a pint of bitter cost 2/- (10p). There was another pub further down Haverstock Hill called *The Noble Art*, because there was a boxing gym behind it. Originally it had been called *The Load Of Hay,* then *The Hill* [now returned to the original name *The Load of Hay* –Ed.].

I was working in the City and used to take the train from the former Primrose Hill station to Broad Street. Once I had to go to Paris for six weeks and while I was away the flat was burgled and I lost my record player.

I used to go to the Haverstock Hill Odeon, paying 5/6d (27½ p) for a rear stalls ticket: it was a lovely Art Deco cinema with a Compton organ which I heard just once.

The Odeon closed in 1972 and was replaced by Budgens supermarket with a small cinema at the side. I also went to the Swiss Cottage Odeon where the Royal Philharmonic Orchestra gave concerts on Sunday nights.

In 1970 I moved to a studio flat in Duncan House on the corner of Steele's Road and Fellows Road. The rent was £7 a week on top of which I had to pay rates of £2 a week, just about the same as I pay now in Council Tax for a two bedroomed duplex with a patio and a private car park! I used to help out at the old Hampstead Theatre on Tuesday evenings: I loved that portakabin, unlike its modern replacement.

One improvement has been the introduction of the C11 and 168 bus routes: neither Haverstock Hill nor England's Lane had a bus service then.

I've lived in Yorkshire, Surrey and Sussex since those times but have always come back to this area of London and am currently living on the edge of Primrose Hill.

Odeon Haverstock Hill interior featuring the Compton organ, (with enlarged inset) *archive*

PUBS, CLUBS AND ENTERTAINMENT

Odeon Swiss Cottage, 1937, *archive*

Poster for a film screened at
the Odeon Haverstock Hill in 1934

145

BELSIZE Remembered

# The Days of the Classic Cinema
## David S Percy

In the 1960s I spent many enjoyable years as the Chief Projectionist at the Classic cinema on Pond Street, which some readers may also remember became the ABC cinema in the 1970s. The Hampstead Picture Playhouse had opened on this site in August 1913 and was described at the time by the *Daily Chronicle* as "Perhaps the most beautiful cinematograph theatre in London".

Being close to the tram terminus on South End Green and Hampstead Heath railway station, the cinema did excellent business over the years. The theatre was very proud of the velvet-upholstered seats and its very grand interior featuring a richly-ornamented barrel-vaulted ceiling.

It was renamed the Hampstead Playhouse in 1946, and in 1965 it became the Classic Hampstead. After three years the cinema was modernised and I supervised the installation of a much larger proscenium and a new wide screen.

One day we discovered an original poster during the renovations that was located under the floorboards of the manager's office. It was advertising – not exactly air conditioning – but the benefits of an electric fan that brought in "Fresh air from the Heath". The theatre also served afternoon tea to those in the balcony sitting in the twin-seat settees.

The cinema screened a different programme every week on its traditional twin 35mm film projectors powered by old-fashioned carbon arc lamps. Very much a far cry from today's 4K digital cinemas with Dolby surround audio systems! Among the regular local adverts we ran each week was one for Salmon Florist (alas, now long gone) that was located adjacent to Belsize Park tube station.

Jointly with our sister theatre at Piccadilly Circus, the Classic Pond Street hosted the UK première of the ground breaking counterculture movie *Easy Rider* – complete with a specially designed 1960s-style lightshow that played out as an overture on the theatre curtains before each performance. Unfortunately, this fabulous theatre is now gone, having been replaced by an M&S food store with accommodation above.

Every time I pass by I can't help recalling that very special cinema along with the memories of all those wonderful films we screened, including 1960s classics such as *The Graduate, Butch Cassidy and the Sundance Kid, Rosemary's Baby, The Odd Couple, Midnight Cowboy* and *2001: A Space Odyssey*.

PUBS, CLUBS AND ENTERTAINMENT

The Classic cinema in the 1960s, *archive*

South End Green in the 1930s – the Hampstead Picture Playhouse
is just visible to the right of the large tree, *archive*

# Entertainment, Pubs, Restaurants and Cafés

*Robert Labi*

For a time in the late 1960s and the early 1970s *Ye Olde Swiss Cottage* pub (which had a different internal layout, with two very large bars on the ground floor) was quite a gathering point for young people from the area and other parts of north-west London. This was before Camden Town began to develop its own 'scene' and Swiss Cottage was a starting point for some before they went into the West End, to private parties or the Round House in Chalk Farm for its "all-nighters".

In the 1960s and early 70s there were at least four disco/late bars in the Finchley Road tube station area, like the Nordic (upstairs), Voom-Voom (downstairs), the Purple Pussy Cat just off the Finchley Road and La Cage D'Or at the top of Greencroft Gardens, behind John Barnes/Waitrose.

The Country Club was behind Haverstock Hill on land which was built over by Camden Council as part of the Russell Nurseries housing development. Some internet entries on its location are not accurate, it was roughly a bit south of where Aspern Grove is now, but what is true is that it became one of the top, although small, London venues for many emerging artists and groups in the 1960s and early 1970s including Jimi Hendrix, Pink Floyd etc.

In the days when drinking hours were more controlled there were a number of 'private'/'illegal' places to drink alcohol during the old afternoon break when the pubs were closed between 3 and 5.30pm and then after 11pm. There was one in a cellar in Haverstock Hill by Belsize Park tube station, I think underneath the Garner & Pope chemist shop, on the east side where now there are a number of hamburger and pizza places.

In the early 1970s there was a "private" all night drinking establishment, Django's, in Finchley Road, where the O2 shopping centre is now. There was also The Moon and Sixpence all-night café in College Crescent where there was no alcohol but you could drink instant coffee, eat simple food and talk all night long. Its site has now been re-developed as part of a school extension.

Belsize Village had its own social scene in the 1960s centred around the renowned Witch's Cauldron coffee bar, which included an area downstairs in the cellar.

*Ye Olde Swiss Cottage* pub and garden

# Goldilocks Would Live in Belsize Park

## *Stephen Kahn*

If Goldilocks was thinking of relocating to London I'm certain she'd discover that Belsize Park was "just right." I did when I moved here nearly 15 years ago and I've never had reason to change my mind. Then in my mid-50s, my move was prompted by divorce and the need to set up a new home somewhere in London as quickly as possible, but the choice of Belsize Park was dictated by my association of the area with the good times I enjoyed as a teenager in the 1960s.

Back then Belsize Village was the focus of a mini-'youth scene' – a place to pick up on the appeal of several Saturday night parties in easy walking distance. First at the Witch's Cauldron coffee bar and then a little later across the road at the *Belsize Tavern* – both now long gone.

Occasionally, Saturday night would find us at the Country Club behind Belsize Park tube station, the music venue next to the tennis club. There I saw the Rolling Stones so early in their careers that they carried their own equipment from a van parked on Haverstock Hill.

Belsize Park had a good Swinging Sixties vibe, but would it suit the older me? This simple answer was a resounding 'yes'. It ticks all the boxes and more. It is brilliantly located, well-served by public transport. London's lungs – Hampstead Heath, Primrose Hill, and Regents Park – are all in walking distance.

With our post office restored and the Belsize Library re-opened most amenities are on hand. The shops are not the cheapest but then I suppose neither are their rents.

The surrounding areas have much to be proud of but what is unique about Belsize Park is its sense of space. There seems to be more sky here, a boon when so much else in the capital seems claustrophobic.

BELSIZE Remembered

# Soul Music at the Witch's Cauldron
## *Mel Wright*

It was 1966 and I was nineteen years old. I had not long returned from a short stint drumming with a band, playing at an American Air Force base in Orléans, France – much to my dad's dismay as I'd given up a secure office job to do so. When I returned to London I was keen to find something new. Three of us who had started a youth club beat group in 1963 decided to form a soul band. The Barrel House Band was inspired by hearing the cool sounds of Georgie Fame and Zoot Money at Klooks Kleek club at West Hampstead.

The Witch's Cauldron at No.50 Belsize Lane was a likely cellar dive for our new venture. Its bistro/coffee bar atmosphere felt significantly more sophisticated than playing between bingo sessions at working men's clubs around Harlesden and Willesden. I was immediately attracted to the Cauldron's arty posters and tables with candlelit wine bottles, also dreamy student girls looking like Jean Shrimpton, reading Penguin paperbacks and who I imagined lived in nearby Belsize bedsits. The club had a folksy feel, with regular appearances by Ram Holder Brothers, John Le Mont, The Mox and The Frugal Sound, who recorded for Pye Records, and did a cover of The Beatles' *Norwegian Wood*.

The Cauldron had a slightly intellectual appeal but it also attracted a teenage audience, particularly for weekend sessions of pop and R&B groups: The Clique, The Jet Set, The Soul Mates, The Pieces Fit, Idle Hands and C-Jam Blues.

We, the Barrel House Band, were booked for a mid-week residency and in February we arrived with our equipment in an LEB works van driven by our organist. Our line-up of vocalist, trumpet, sax, organ, guitar, bass and drums scrambled down the very narrow staircase to the club with all our gear. The first challenge was to fit my new silver sparkle Ajax drum kit on to the cramped stage. As the music started our mates led the dancing and we blasted the place out with our repertoire of Ray Charles, Otis Redding, Wilson Pickett and James Brown numbers.

The Cauldron's manager Gerry was pleased that we had attracted a good crowd. During the break we sneaked across the road to the *Belsize Tavern* for a pint. This became our regular haunt for a Guinness and a breather from the steaming walls of the club. With an expectation of 'cash on the night' of around ten shillings (50p) each we could afford to down a couple of pints before we were called back on stage.

We enjoyed being part of the Belsize music scene and meeting other musicians, sharing tips and contacts about the gig circuit. As we were going down so well we were invited at short notice to play the Cauldron's showcase gig at Hampstead Town Hall on 5th February. This time we had to hump our equipment up the sweeping, grand, municipal staircase. This spacious public hall with its high level stage gave us room to spread ourselves out and present a soul show for the dancers. We had become friendly with blues player Mox (Gowland) who was also on the bill, and he introduced all the acts. He sat in with us on harmonica and he had a great sound. After our set at the Town Hall I was relaxing in the dressing room when one of the dreamy looking Cauldron girls, a friend of C-Jam Blues, came over and told me that she thought we were very good. I felt that we'd made it! We were becoming popular and not long after we also played at

The Casablanca Club in Broadhurst Gardens alongside The Frugal Sound.

Just as things were going so well for us at the club there was a falling out within the band. We had just done an audition at The Scotch of St James in Mayfair but it hadn't gone well. Our trumpet player proposed changes in our line-up. It resulted in agonizing, divided loyalties and the departure of our singer and organist/van driver. It seemed that we were suddenly pitched from being a hot soul-blues band with a bright future playing the clubs to being a fragmented ensemble. Then, as we were standing outside the Cauldron after a gig, the band's horn players announced they were leaving the band to accompany some visiting American soul singers. Suddenly our residency at the Witch's Cauldron had ended.

Those of us who remained quickly re-formed as we were booked to play at The Purple Pussy Cat, off Finchley Road. All the gigs were now negotiated by me as I had suddenly become the band's fixer. As we did not have a telephone at home, I had to do my fixing by calling from a public telephone box – "Press button A and we might get a gig!" said Ron, our bass player. Ricky who ran The Purple Pussy Cat was confident enough to hype us up in for an advert in *The Jewish Chronicle* as: 'The Most Controversial Sound since The Rolling Stones'. The club also sported the 'Kinkiest Discotheque'!

By early 1967 soul music was petering out as flower power, psychedelia and the summer of love beckoned. The Belsize connection continued with me playing in Shakey Vick's Big City Blues Band at The Blues Thing/Hole in the Ground, a folk cellar beneath an Israeli café in Winchester Road, Swiss Cottage, and later we got a Sunday evening residency with The Nighthawks blues group at *The Three Horseshoes*, Heath Street, Hampstead. But the good old days at the Witch's Cauldron were over.

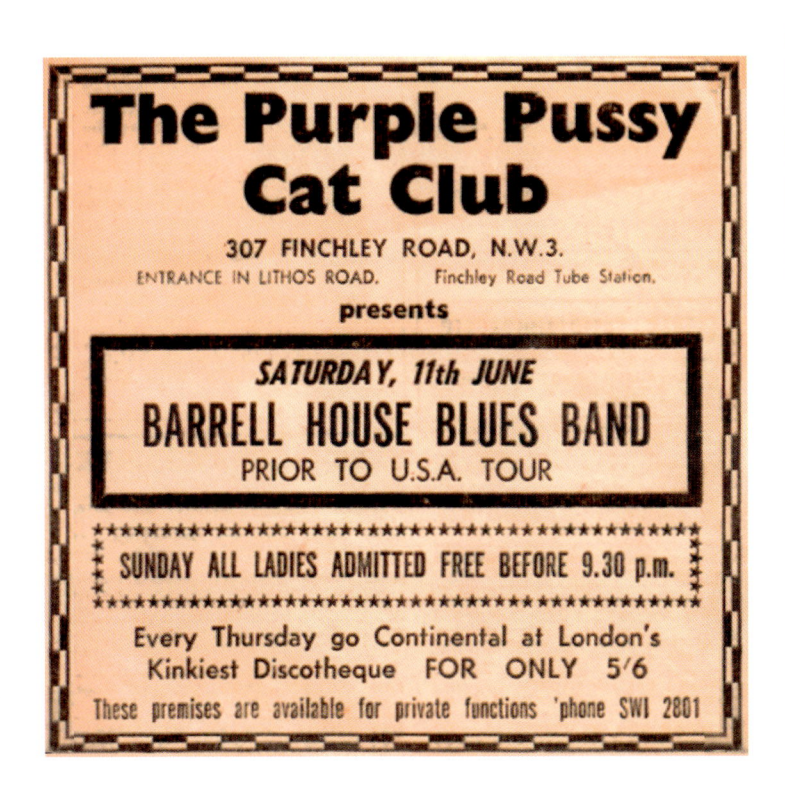

The Barrel House Band at the Witch's Cauldron
Ron Skinner vocals & bass and Mel Wright drums, 1966
*photo provided by M Wright*

BELSIZE Remembered

# The Siege of The Load of Hay

*Barry Ewart*

There have been times in my life when I've been so broke that I've fantasised about robbing a bank, ramraiding an ATS machine or heaving a brick through a jeweller's window; but even at my lowest financial ebb I never considered an armed blag on a sleepy little carpet retailer's in broad daylight. Maybe I don't think 'outside the box' enough, but somebody did. I know it for a fact because I was there and so were several more witnesses, although their accounts may differ somewhat from mine.

The Monday Club in *The Load of Hay* was in full session. Gerry the Carpet, a regular lunchtime customer, had just gone back to work in the carpet shop opposite, replete with a Dekko the Brekko take away special. Gerry's partner in the shop, Tom, would be in for his half pint and sandwich in a few moments.

Or so we thought.

A sweating John the Post came to the bar and settled beside Jimmy Mac, Communist and former shop steward and an immigrant from Birkenhead.

"Allright John"? asked Jimmy Mac.

"Yeah, just finished me walk."

"Well it keeps you off the streets I suppose."

I think the GPO induction course must espouse Willy Nilly Postman from 'Under Milk Wood' as the paragon of postal virtue because John the Post then proceeded to describe to everybody exactly what he'd popped through letter boxes that morning, even quoting greetings on their postcards, verbatim. The Post was a recent recruit to the GPO having previously been known as John the Pot. The Pot's supersonic elevation from glass collector in *The Steeles*, through the smoke to the stratospheric height of manager was the stuff of pub legend, though he was never referred to as John the Manager. Perhaps he developed vertigo from such a steep ascent because he left *The Steeles* and joined the Post Office, which career move immediately awarded an extra consonant to his nickname.

The pub began to fill through the early afternoon and weekend hangovers started to fade. A guitar was produced in one corner and an ad hoc jamming session was underway when a burly flak-jacketed copper complete with automatic rifle exploded through the door and announced that nobody was to leave the premises until further notice. The image of gobsmacked faces will stay with me for ever. How surreal was this? The police ordering us to stay in the pub under threat of armed violence! The ensuing silence was broken when Belfast Willy lurched in from the toilets and slap into the arms of Action Man. Clutching the policeman for support Willy babbled "Are you for real, amigo, or what"? Belfast Willy is a former Irish Guardsman and his speech is peppered with phrases from John Wayne and Dean Martin Westerns or quotes from De Niro/Pacino-type Wise Guys. Regardless, most people haven't a clue what Willy's saying at the best of times but mid Monday Club the policeman would have had no chance. No problem to one of London's finest. "STAY THERE AND SHUT THE FUCK UP!!!"

Willy was dumped into a bench seat and the policeman strode out and positioned himself on the top step of three outside the elaborately frosted glass door.

Somewhere up above a helicopter droned.

The Monday Club is not easily bullied. Above the general hubbub of voices I heard phrases like "police state"..."infringement of civil liberties"...and "Maggie Thatcher!"...this last with more venom than the Iron Lady usually merited from the Monday Club, or indeed the 1922 Committee. At this point I recall thinking that I must have committed a host of cardinal sins in a previous existence. Why else was I locked in a pub with this selection of punters? Somewhere, I thought, there is a karma comedian. Rebellion was fomenting and the chief insurgents were those who

The *Load of Hay*, c.1900
*archive*

always had to be prised from their stools at last orders. Now they all had unassailable reasons for quitting the pub at 4pm.

John the Post, normally such a reliable punter until well into the evening, insisted that his huge gay Alsatian dog, Max, would be pining for him. Jimmy Mac started spouting the Communist Manifesto and John the Drum, having organised the collection of his daughter from school on the pub phone, demanded a bar tab for the duration. And to think I used to complain about working the 'graveyard' shift. Sean the Actor talked himself into a state of apoplexy. No Fascist regime was going to keep the greatest Hamlet in living memory (Sheffield Crucible ca.1960) locked in a pub. He grabbed his Sainsbury's carrier bags and made a beeline for the door and if I hadn't intercepted him in the nick of time he'd have barged out and tipped the copper headlong down the steps.

I eased him back into his seat, collected a few glasses on my way back and nearly dropped the lot as Belfast Willy slammed his fist on the table and roared "JUST LIKE THE ALAMO...NO SURRENDER!!!"

Mobile phones were only just on the market but there was at least one in the pub that day because snippets of information from the outside world were soon circulating around the bar. There had been a robbery at Tom and Gerry's carpet shop! The felons had fled into Steele's Road, the whole area was swarming with armed police and their dogs were rooting through local gardens. Haverstock Hill had been cordoned off from a point just south of *The Load of Hay* upwards to England's Lane, so the *Sir Richard Steele*, almost opposite, had also been besieged.

A robbery in a carpet shop? What flawed genius masterminded that? Who pays readies for carpets? At this time we didn't know that Carpet Gerry had walked right into the scene and found poor old Tom badly manhandled and trussed to a chair. At some stage in the ensuing negotiations Gerry found a chance to boot one of the two thugs in the balls, whereupon they saw fit to scarper.

Back in *The Load of Hay* somebody shouted "Where's John the Post?" Answer came there none. He'd legged it through the kitchen, over the alley wall and garden-hopped until he'd broken the siege cordon.

We didn't notice that the shadow of the policeman had disappeared until new faces appeared in the bar. By this time Belfast Willy was involved in a smoochy dance with himself to his beloved Dean Martin, two clowns were attempting "Chopsticks" on the battered piano and John the Drum had run up a tab in double figures at £1 per pint.

You can talk of Leningrad, Sydney Street and the Iranian Embassy, but in the pantheon of sieges *The Load of Hay* is up there.

BELSIZE Remembered

# The Haverstock Arms

*Paul Birtill*

My first memory of Belsize Park was of marching up Haverstock Hill with other London Anarchists, chanting and surrounded by Police.

It was of course the Anarchists' annual Bash the Rich march, and that year, 1985, they chose Belsize Park to demonstrate. I remember thinking it was a lovely part of London, very leafy with wide pavements and quaint little coffee shops. I had no idea I'd get a council flat here a few years later. I moved into Parkhill Road in the spring of 1988 and my local pub became *The Haverstock Arms* on Haverstock Hill, known later as *The Havers*. Sadly, it closed in 2012, but I was a regular for many years and had some great times there.

The pub was popular with many famous actors, including the late Ronnie Fraser and Simon Ward. I also met Robert Powell and the Radio 1 DJ Chris Evans there. In fact the publican Andrew Carey appeared regularly on Chris Evans' live TV show TGIF (Thank God It's Friday).

There used to be a wonderful Irish Folk night on Sundays; their Sunday roast was the best around and their beer wasn't bad either. In later years it became a B&B with very reasonably priced rooms. It also had a roof garden terrace, lovely to sit out in during the summer. I remember one New Year's Eve it stayed open all night and I didn't get home until 9am the next morning.

Most of all, though, I used to like sitting on one of the many benches outside with my pint and just watch the world go by. I do miss it.

*The Haverstock Arms* in the late 1980s
*photo provided by P Birtill*

PUBS, CLUBS AND ENTERTAINMENT

# Memories of Upper Park Road and The Haverstock Arms
## Julia Mathews

I think that Upper Park Road and this part of Belsize Park is one of the most beautiful parts of London. Very lively and friendly people, it's extraordinary, like a village, and it's amazing how many people greet us when we walk along the road.

But the most marvellous thing about the street was *The Haverstock Arms* that stood on the corner with Haverstock Hill, which I had always loved because of the horse-drawn brewer's dray painted on the side of the building.

Very much a local pub, it was most often absolutely packed. Andrew, the publican, was known to everybody, and he knew all the locals, even those who never went into his pub, because he was always outside saying hello to people.

*The Haverstock Arms*, c.1955 NBHT CC BY-SA

*The Havers* in 2012, previously *The Haverstock Arms*

The building is now the Haverstock Hotel, 2016

155

BELSIZE Remembered

# Villains in the Tunnel and Rebels in the Crown

*Barry Ewart*

The advent of all-day opening was inevitable and welcome but oh, how I lament the passing of the 'lock-in'. Whether by this name or another one like 'afters' or, in the North-East, 'stoppybacks', you felt special when the guvnor sidled up and whispered "If you're staying, move to the end of the bar" as he ushered the hoi polloi out into a foul, rainy afternoon. This meant you were accepted, part of the family; at home.

Daytime lock-ins had a different flavour from night sessions. There was a delicious feeling of superiority amounting to smugness when the curtains were re-opened and the doors unbolted to admit punters not favoured with the earlier invitation. The known 'afters' pubs didn't extend such invitations on a daily basis. It was more an unspoken sort of arrangement, dependent upon the guvnor's moods. Regulars developed a sixth sense as to which pub was most likely to oblige and trusted to instinct that they were perched on a stool in the right bar at 2.30pm.

On unsuccessful days there were the infamous private members' clubs, a euphemism for only just legal shebeens. One such was the Tunnel Club, known to some as the Villains' Club, adjacent to Belsize Park tube station. On the one occasion when I was present it was stocked with scurrilous-looking Glaswegian heavies in sharp Italian suits containing razor blades stitched in to their lapels, former world boxing champions, and well-known actors of the day who couldn't be bothered or weren't capable of cabbing it to one of the legitimate luvvies' clubs in Soho.

So afternoon lock-ins are history, and night-time sessions are not what they were since the police have realised the futility of taking fictitious names and addresses of hapless punters in the wee small hours. The naughty pleasure derived from keeping the singing down for fear of a heavy knock on the door has been taken away.

My favourite lock-in house of those times is now razed to the ground and where it stood the shell of a block of luxury flats grows daily higher. Its most recent incarnation was, by some quirk of fate, a solicitors' office, though the tatty old sign, 'The Crown' still hung outside as I passed it daily and I wondered what its bright young clerks, certainly gastro-pubbers, would have made of the roisterous scenes that took place there in the eighties when Belfast Paul and Cavan Lucy presided.

From Friday night to 5am on a Monday seemed like one uninterrupted session. If the curtains were closed a coded rap on the window with a coin would gain admission to a recognised face at any hour and once inside there was barely room to lift a pint. There would be a card game around one large table, pool matches in the small bar and musicians and singing everywhere. Any man foolish enough to fall asleep in his chair was inviting the landlady to demonstrate her artistic nature with the contents of her make-up bag. Many's the hulking Connemara navvy I've seen stir from his slumber with a face like Julian Clary on acid and plod through the bar to a waiting taxi, blissfully unaware of his make-over.

One Sunday afternoon in particular sticks in my memory. The doors were locked, the heavy drapes pulled to, the air was blue with smoke, accents from Ireland's thirty-two counties bounced from wall to wall and the craic, as they say, was ninety. Doyle had twice been called to the phone and twice resumed his seat at the card table. There came a tap on the window, the door was opened and Mrs Doyle appeared holding a plate boasting a Sunday roast and all the trimmings. She was at the card table in a flash as bodies parted like the Red Sea, poured the dinner over Doyle's head and without a word she was gone. Doyle removed his hat since the gravy was dripping from the brim into his Guinness and continued dealing. Well, I was familiar with the expression "Fan the flames of love with the bellows of indifference", but this beat all.

Then came the hard knock. That knock!

"Quick!!" yelled Squaddy Dave, the cockney barman, "Dahn the cellar, 'urry up!!", with which some fifty or sixty Irish men and women made their way behind the bar, through the trapdoor and down into the bowels of the pub. Despite it being a tried and tested routine this manoeuvre was no threat to the Edinburgh tattoo since many of the punters were old and infirm, some very portly and most completely legless. Eventually the hatch was closed and Squaddy Dave admitted a few uniforms.

The police surveyed the detritus of full pints of Guinness, cigarettes still burning in ashtrays and Doyle's lunch dripping from the card table. Bang to rights as they say. Squaddy expected the usual production of a notebook, the licking of a pencil and the checking of the till to confirm the time of the last transaction. Just as he opened his mouth to utter some paltry excuse the opening lines of Carrickfergus issued forth in a high tenor from somewhere beneath the soles of his boots, followed by "SSSHHHH!!!" and then "Ah bollix to them!!!". The coppers glanced at the floor, then at Squaddy and finally at each other, shook their heads in a knowing sort of way, turned on their heels and exited stage left. Moments later the bar was heaving and Squaddy was rushed off his feet again.

They just don't make Sundays like that any more.

Believed to be the door to the Tunnel Club in the 1980s located to the left of the entrance to Belsize Park tube station

BELSIZE Remembered

# The Washington
## *Terry Tidey*

The first time I came to *The Washington* on England's Lane, I was running *The Anglers* in Teddington, Middlesex. We had received a phone call asking if I was interested in running *The Washington* in Hampstead/Belsize Park. My wife and I walked into the pub, which was quite busy that day. Immediately a group of guys got talking to me who play cricket – I play cricket too, it's my passion. They convinced me it was a good idea to come to *The Washington* and run the pub, which I decided to do – that was in the summer of 1988.

The first time that I had ever heard of Daniel Tidey [the developer from Washington, Sussex who built much of central Belsize including *The Washington*] was when I received a letter from a lady called Meryl Rafferty who lived in Walberswick in Suffolk.

I now know that Daniel Tidey is my Great, Great, Great Grandfather. I don't have a photograph of Daniel Tidey himself, but I do have one of Daniel Tidey Junior with his sons around him.

Many American visitors come into the pub due to its name *The Washington*, and their first reaction is "Wow!" The mirrors at the rear of the bar have been there for over 150 years and so have the bar fittings. Many of the cornices are also original.

The pub is the centre of the local community, and to think you are only ten minutes from the middle of London, Belsize has so much to offer, it's the perfect place to live!

*Daniel Tidey Jr with his sons*
photo provided by T Tidey

*The Washington* in 1978, *archive*

PUBS, CLUBS AND ENTERTAINMENT

Interior views of *The Washington*, 2012

BELSIZE Remembered

# Mary Anne Sheehan Dillon 1884-1970
## Anthony Dillon

Mary Anne Dillon was a remarkable woman for her era – a time when women had only recently acquired the right to own property and were not generally expected to be in business. By the early years of the First World War, she had two sons and owned two shops in Tralee, the County Town of County Kerry, in Ireland. One of the shops was a milliners and Mary would recall how she travelled to London with £50 in gold to buy stock, eventually even purchasing surplus hat bases from Selfridges, where she held a trade account until her death. Her husband, Jerome, formerly employed by the Post Office had enlisted and was a Sergeant Major in the Royal Munster Fusiliers. Having seen action in Gallipoli, and later on the Western Front he had returned alive but 'shell-shocked'.

In 1920, when one shop was burnt out by the 'black & tans', an unruly and brutal British security force, she sold up and moved with her family to Notting Hill, London. There she bought a shop and a house in Oxford Gardens where she started in the business of serviced accommodation, providing lodging and meals for mainly young men, who would have been part of the rapidly-growing workforce required by London's businesses. Then in 1926 she sold up in Notting Hill and bought No.44 Belsize Park where she opened the Avoca House Hotel, acquiring adjacent properties as success allowed. Eventually, the hotel provided 120 bedrooms and extended from 39 to 46 Belsize Park. Many of the 'bridges' connecting the houses could still be seen until recent redevelopment. Meanwhile, she was also buying properties around the neighbourhood where she would install a housekeeper and a maid to continue the serviced accommodation business, with the main hotel able to provide the food service.

Clearly, Mary was an astute businesswoman and her success was in the main part attributable to hard work, but she was the first to admit that she had also been very lucky. Lucky in business, maybe; tragically, of her five children, Deborah died of diphtheria as a baby and James was knocked down and killed by a horse-drawn cart before her move to Belsize Park. However, she did see her other three children, Jerome, Patrick and Eddie grow up and all of them go on to University or College.

By the 1960s, Mary had retired, with the business expanded to include hotels in Folkestone and Broadstairs, four further houses in Belsize Park itself, and properties in Buckland Crescent, Belsize Avenue, Belsize Lane, Lancaster Grove and Lancaster Drive.

Mary is buried in Fortune Green Cemetery.

Extracted from *The Kerryman*, October 1959

Mary Anne Dillon outside the Avoca House Hotel, late 1920s
*photo provided by A Dillon*

REMARKABLE CHARACTERS

Dillons Hotel, No.21 Belsize Park in 2016

View from near the Avoca House Hotel in the 1920s, *archive*

BELSIZE Remembered

# My Mother Eileen Hunter
## Wendy Richards

Eileen, born in 1903, was my amazing mother. A resident in Belsize for four decades, she was everyone's favourite neighbour with her practical, talented, loving and giving nature. The skills she learned at night school in Holmes Road were put to work in the homes of less capable friends. She always seemed to be mending curtains, up ladders hanging them, and up more ladders painting and hanging wallpaper. She was always a bundle of energy and such fun to be with, a fount of wisdom and of gifts to us all of home-made wine – really powerful stuff, heavy to carry down three flights of stairs in bottles and demijohns.

She began making wine when we had a glut of rhubarb in the garden and progressed to making it out of everything, including rice, potatoes, even bread. Judges awarded her several prizes, never guessing that she had combined wines from a wide variety of sources. We loved old recipes like Spennymoors Orange, in which orange peel was roasted before a sweet sherry emerged. My daughter ordered that variety for her wedding breakfast!

In the General Strike mother volunteered to drive ambulances. Eileen loved driving, especially long distances, and went to night school to learn car maintenance. She was an excellent teacher and taught her grand-daughters to drive by letting them take the wheel on trips to Devon. She lent her car to a learner driver friend, and while the learning took place Eileen took a round-the-world cruise on a French liner, where she gave hair and beauty treatments.

She drove over vast tracts of Australia and said I would have been horrified to see her covered with red dust. On returning to the UK she found her landlady had changed the locks and put her possessions out on the landing. Undaunted, she and a friend rented No.8 Parkhill Road, which had been owned by a podiatrist and set about completely redecorating, even to upholstering the armchairs and sofa.

Mother had green fingers and grew herbs in her home-made oak window boxes. She also had a gigantic ivy that grew the entire height along the stairs. In its honour she chose ivy wallpaper, so it looked like a jungle as you opened the front door. But the Toby jugs she had been collecting looked so much like the villainous landlady that she threw them all away.

Mother was named Citizen of the Year by Camden in 1980, and was rewarded by having her telephone located in a more convenient place. That proved less than convenient as neighbours would keep her chatting about all their woes for so long that she'd be eating her food cold. They craved her wisdom and the kindness of a listening ear. We bought her a warming plate hoping that she'd manage to eat her food hot again.

The *Ham&High* ran an article about Lady Drivers and mother featured in it. They also had a piece on "Death of popular lollipop lady". Mother read her obituary on her return from holiday. She had been to Hell in Scandinavia but had assured us she had a return ticket! She knew about all the children she shepherded as lollipop lady at Fitzjohn's School and always had help for harassed mums – safety pins, lifts advice, anything. The teachers knew she was utterly reliable. Actually, to get the job she had falsified her age by 10 years ("a lady's age is no one's business, unless she's committed a criminal offence" she would say). Being a tough outdoor girl she thrived in even the coldest weather. I would knit her string vests to keep her warm. How proud I felt of her, and only hope I told her so.

When she eventually died in 1984, we found her Nature Diaries spanning 30 years full of joy and observations. Her last diaries left this poem of hope for us to find:

Think of –
Taking hold of a hand
The hand of God
Passing thro' storm and tempest
To a perpetual calm
Breathing a new air
Celestial air
Stepping ashore and finding it
Heaven
Waking up and finding it
HOME

Eileen Hunter

No.8 Parkhill Road, early spring, 2017

BELSIZE Remembered

# The Music Man
## *Naomi Stadlen*

Does anyone remember the old "music man", who used to stand playing his violin every morning under the great plane tree, which is still there on the little triangle of land opposite Winchester Road, where it meets Eton Avenue? He had a cloth cap into which we used to drop coins.

I went to St Mary's Town and Country School at 38-40 Eton Avenue, run by Mrs Elisabeth Paul, a German-Jewish refugee. So my daily walk to school was along Finchley Road, then over to Swiss Cottage where there were no traffic lights at that time, just one lone policeman who used to stop the traffic when enough people had gathered to cross over. Once past the entrance to Swiss Cottage Underground station, I could usually hear the violin, very clear and cheering, usually playing something classical. My brother and I would hurry past and the violinist would give us a wave of recognition with his bow, and a huge smile. He had white curly hair, a brown jacket, and a threadbare full-length coat when it was cold.

I thought him eternal – but he isn't there now. I do hope someone reading this remembers him too.

St Mary's Town and Country School was an independent, non-denominational, co-educational progressive day and boarding school, founded in Belsize Park in 1937 – the school closed at the end of 1982
*Photo from Kumiko Takahashi*

REMARKABLE CHARACTERS

The great plane tree, Eton Avenue, autumn, 2016

BELSIZE Remembered

# Belsize Park Chocolaterie

*Ellie Beutel*

I am from Berlin and arrived here during the war. Initially I was a domestic help, starting as a charwoman at a chocolate shop in Belsize Grove, where Hadleigh Residential is located now. There were two businesses in that space: one was the chocolate shop and the other was a laundry which took in clothes to be sent away to be washed.

One day when I was cleaning the shop the owner asked me to help him with making chocolates, a skill he had learnt in Germany. Later he somehow got me a permit to work as his assistant and officially employed me for 6d an hour in 1940. His wife and their baby became like my family and they offered me a hot meal with them in the evening for 6d.

I lived in Adelaide Road in a little room for a short time, paying 7 shillings a week. The bathroom was upstairs and I had to put in tuppence if I wanted to have a bath. I went to the shop every morning to work, and on the way I walked up Primrose Gardens and then along Belsize Grove, past Holmefield Court. I thought if only I could afford a little room in this block of flats – but I couldn't manage it on my wages.

The chocolates were made at the back of the shop. After a while we needed more production so he took on two other girls: my friends Trude and Traute. We lived as a family.

Downstairs there was a huge basement and we felt very safe there during the air raids, not realising that if a bomb hit it we would all be drowned and gassed because all the pipes were in the basement. We were lucky when a bomb fell into the basement next door where the restaurant Chez Nous is now. Customers regularly asked if they could come and stay in the basement. When the bombs stopped everyone went back to their homes. The owner sent his wife and baby to America to be safe, and around 1942 he joined them. We three girls took over the shop, paying him whatever the business was worth at the time.

After we took over the business Traute and I managed the 28 shillings per week and rented studio flat No.98 in Holmefield Court. We bought a couch for 5 shillings from Lawson's second hand shop in Haverstock Hill. We often had parties in our flats during the air raids and played music loudly so that we couldn't hear the aircraft. On D-Day we all went up to the roof and watched thousands of planes passing over to the Continent. Everybody knew everybody then, there was a lovely community feeling in and around the area. I remember there was a gas lamp outside Garrett Anderson Maternity Home which was near Holmefield Court, and every night a man came with a long stick and lit the lamp.

Eventually Trude got married and left to live in the US. Traute also married and went to live in Brazil. So I became the sole owner of the chocolate shop, now named 'Blue-Red Chocolates Ltd' – the chocolate box lid was rectangular, with one half blue and the other half red.

People came from everywhere to buy our chocolates, which were hardly available anywhere then. A financier had an interest in a big chocolate factory in the country and he supplied us with raw materials, so we could just manage during the war. After the war chocolates from Belgium and Holland began to be available so our customers came in to the shop to say we don't come as customers anymore but as friends.

SHOPS AND SHOPPING

Ellie Beutel (right) with
Traute and Trude (left) in 1945
*photo provided by E Beutel*

Built in 1826, and originally known as Haverstock Terrace, this fine group stands opposite Holmefield Court and Gilling Court on Belsize Grove

BELSIZE Remembered

# Butchers' Shops on England's Lane
## *Bob Enright*

Barrett's Butchers started at No.16 England's Lane in around 1890. The shop I am in now, at No.40 which is also Barrett's, used to belong to a butcher called T Gurney Randall.

When I first came here there were 27 butcher shops in NW3 – I got down to being the only one [until recently: a new one opened on Rosslyn Hill in about 2010 –Ed].

When people did their shopping years ago, they used to come to England's Lane and spend 15 to 20 minutes buying their meat, "Good morning Bob", "Good morning Bill". In those days it would be a morning's work to do the weekend shopping.

I always sell Orkney beef and Orkney lamb, to me it's probably the best. Customers don't buy the cheaper cuts as they used to any more, customers buy two pieces of steak, lamb chops, something that's easy to cook. People are much busier now than they were years ago.

I must say it's been an absolute pleasure to serve all my customers over the years.

England's Lane shops, c.1900, *archive*

SHOPS AND SHOPPING

T Gurney Randall the butcher (just by the horse) around 1905, *archive*

---

By Special Appointment to H.R.H. the Prince of Wales.

## T. G. RANDALL,
### ☞ BUTCHER, ☜
ENGLAND LANE, & 93, HAVERSTOCK HILL,
BELSIZE PARK, N.W.

*WELCH MUTTON, Spécialité for the Season.*

T. G. R., while thanking the public for their liberal patronage during the past 13 years, hopes by persevering attention to his business to merit their continued support.

*T. G. RANDALL respectfully invites a visit to his Establishment,*
ENGLAND LANE, BELSIZE PARK, N.W.

## Belsize Shops in the 1960s
### Françoise Findlay

During the 1960s I remember pushing my baby boy in his pram from King Henry's Road to do my shopping at J. Sainsbury and Mac Fisheries in the Belsize shopping parade. There were two Sainsbury shops on the parade near where Leverton & Sons is now. They were not even adjacent shops, one was between Glenloch Road and Howitt Road and the other on the south side of Howitt Road.

I don't remember which was which but one sold dairy products and meat and the other was dry groceries. It was necessary to queue at each counter to be served which took time because all the items had to be cut, weighed and measured out. Payment was at the cash desk where one queued again. This process was then repeated at the other Sainsbury shop down the road. Meanwhile the pram, with the baby, was parked outside on the pavement.

My husband Paul grew up in Lambolle Road and remembers being sent to Coleman's in Belsize Lane to buy paraffin for their heaters.

We both recall the delicatessen in England's Lane, Bona's, and what was then exotic, Continental produce. There was a barrel with pickled cucumbers by the door, salamis and sausages hanging up, cream cheese and halva. The shop was close to the corner where a very fine branch of Barclays Bank occupied what is now Starbucks and I recall Miss Mackenzie perched there behind the mahogany counter on a high stool. Allchin & Co, the chemist, has retained its 1900s corner shop front but sadly the splendid original shelving and counters were ripped out and I was so shocked by this vandalism that I vowed never to return.

There was a baker that became a branch of the Aerated Bread Company – ABC – on the corner of Adelaide Road and on the opposite corner was the chemist run by Mr Brown. There were two greengrocers, a grocer, fish shop, draper and a butcher. Mr Evans and his sister ran the tobacconist/newsagent/sweet shop, and on the corner of King Henry's Road an off licence. There was an electrical shop, an upholsterers and the Primrose Hairdressing Salon. Opposite the parade, now replaced by two matching houses, was Leonard Walker's studio, at No.151. Leonard Walker was a stained glass artist of international repute who built his studio in 1901 and lived there until his death in 1964 aged about 90. He recalled my family home when first built in 1908 as a stable with horses and carriage. He didn't believe in using sheets of coloured glass but mixed plain glass with pigments in a giant cauldron to create his own colours and textures. After his death the fashion photographer Brian Duffy moved in.

Until the early 1960s the houses along the two sides of King Henry's Road mirrored each other. Most were in multi occupancy, many were boarding houses. The exception was No.143, the home of Ernest Read, who did so much to promote classical music for children with his concerts.

By 1964 Eton College had allowed the houses in the area to become extremely run down, with the result that the Italianate stuccoed houses along both sides of Adelaide Road, the south side of Fellows Road, the shopping parade, the North side of King Henry's Road were all demolished to make way for the Chalcots Estate, the mix of houses and tower blocks that exist today.

SHOPS AND SHOPPING

Belsize Parade, c.1906 (J. Sainsbury fourth shop from left)
– the parade little changed in 2011

171

BELSIZE Remembered

# Shops on Haverstock Hill
## Jean Clarke

I remember a small J. Sainsbury grocery store opposite the station and they had a butchers shop a few doors along. Dewhurst's the butchers also had a shop in the parade. There was a chemist where Boots is now and a bookshop where Daunt Books is located today. Grodzinski the Jewish bakery was closed on Saturday but open Sunday so we all had fresh bread on the Sabbath. Eventually a laundrette arrived although I think most of us did our washing by hand at home. I was very generous with my washing line, allowing everyone to dry their clothes in the garden.

There was a small delicatessen run by a very nice Asian man, next to the station. He very kindly cashed cheques for us when we ran out of money at weekends. This was before debit cards and cash points. I can't remember the man's name but we were all dependent on him.

Belsize Stores Haverstock Hill, c.1912, *archive*
the original shopfront is still intact
the shop is currently occupied by B&R Carpets

Belsize Fruit Stores, 179 Haverstock Hill around 1930, *archive*

# Remembering the Old Shops

## Judith Nasatyr

## Anthony Wills

There have been many changes to the shopping facilities in Belsize and the Village. I recall there were two small J. Sainsbury shops on Haverstock Hill – one sold dry goods, cleaning materials etc., while the other sold groceries and had a delicatessen and cheese counter. When they closed my husband bought the marble delicatessen counter intending to make coffee or garden tables with it. It took six strong men to carry the counter to our house in Belsize Avenue where it languished unused for more than thirty years. When I moved in 2012, a decorator who had done work for me took it to his house in France. Already part of it is in use for making bread.

It is heartening that several of the shops on England's Lane are still there:

Allchin & Co the pharmacy, the stationers, the washeteria, the ironmongers [alas no more –Ed], and of course Barrett's the butchers: not forgetting the Indian restaurant and *The Washington* pub.

I believe there was a Viennese restaurant at the end of Elizabeth Mews but I may be mistaken.

Closed J. Sainsbury shop, Haverstock Hill, 1974
*Photo: Henry Grant*

Allchin & Co Pharmacy with its original shopfront and fittings, c.1900, *archive*

BELSIZE Remembered

# Adelaide Community Gardens
## *Glenys McDougall & Janie Shorter*

Adelaide Community Gardens comprise a secret garden and allotments, diverse in nature, where approximately half an acre of garden plots are hidden between the houses of Adelaide Road and Fellows Road – plots dedicated to vegetable and fruit growing, others to flowers. Mature apple, plum and pear trees, a wild garden with ponds and beehives. Polytunnels for bringing on young plants. A small piece of pleasure and calm in the middle of our busy city.

The gardens were originally created by Sister Judith Hinchliffe, who was inspired by concern for the mental and spiritual welfare of local residents, after two suicides in nearby tower blocks. She believed that if people were given a plot to cultivate, it would bring real benefit to their lives. She started campaigning to persuade Camden Council to allow her to establish a community garden on the site and eventually, on the 17th May 1980, the gardens were officially opened.

At this time, Sopna Begum, a current member, was a young child who lived in the basement of No.74 Adelaide Road and remembers that "It was a tarmaced area where we were allowed to play sometimes, and one day big trucks of earth were brought in, and then it was divided into plots."

Once the allotments were established, Sister Judith was tireless in her efforts to raise funds for the gardens until the late 80s. Early contributions came from InterAction, the Hampstead Wells and Camden Estate, and even a greenhouse was funded by the DHSS.

One long-standing member, Jyoti Hardy, recalls "the guts, the power and dedication of those early members to hang on to what they had started".

Francis Radford, a founder member, remembers that "We raised funds with jumble sales at places like *the Winch*. We also made hand-crafted needlework and pottery gifts. In the early days chickens and ducks were reared in the gardens and there was a large rubber ring that acted as a duck pond. Sometimes eggs were sold to swell the funds. We used to meet in a little Nissen hut in Adelaide Road that was the nursery and on one occasion, perched on tiny chairs, we hosted a meeting with the film crew who made the BBC television documentary *The 31 Bus*."

Later in the 1980s there was a threat of demolition as plans for the development of the Edwardian houses in Adelaide Road were drawn up. The architect John Summerson was very influential in the fight to preserve the land. In 2003, as part of our community links, members helped to create a garden for the residents of St Margaret's Older People's Care Home in West Heath Road, Hampstead.

A much missed member of our gardens is Neville Wilson, who for many years was the central axis around which the gardens moved. Until ill health prevented him he could be found in the gardens every day, making structures, repairing and maintaining all manner of things, even when he had given up his own plot. Above all he was the link between all the members of the gardens. The lack of a common language was no deterrent to Neville. He was a great communicator.

The Bangladeshi gardeners have been an integral part of the community gardens since its inception. They grow the most wonderful vines with large courgette-like flowers that produce large gourds that need to be supported on very strong structures, as well as coriander, mustard, many varieties of beans and amaranth, a spinach-like vegetable called 'doogi'.

In 2010, under the leadership of architect Jeff Travers, a Bangladeshi garden was created at the Hampton Court Palace Flower Show. It featured many of the structures used and plants grown by Mrs Khanom and other members of the Bangladeshi community. We are very proud that the garden was awarded a silver medal.

SPECIAL PLACES

Today the gardens boast a clubhouse, an eco-loo and a wild garden with several beehives. Each year in May or June there is an Open Day with a plant sale and delicious home-made culinary treats. The gardens are managed by a team elected by our membership and we all pay a nominal rent for our plots. New members are most welcome and whilst on the waiting list may wish to become associate members. They can then enjoy the gardens and contribute to the common good by assisting on our clean-up days.

The gardens are hidden between the houses of Adelaide Road and Fellows Road

Adelaide Community Gardens

175

BELSIZE Remembered

# Like Grandmother Used to Grow
## *Tamara Cincik*

In June 2007 I was given my allotment plot in Antrim Grove. What an oasis, tucked behind a children's playground! As soon as I knew I was top of the waiting list for the next plot, I'd go up the path, stare through the gate and wonder at the secret garden which lay behind it.

Having a key into this garden has been magical. Arriving in June, I'd missed the main spring planting opportunities, but there were strawberries to be picked, an artichoke to revive and beans to plant. Elsa, who'd had the plot before me, had loved and tended it well, despite her advanced age. As I dug up planks of wood and concrete slabs she'd laid to help her to walk around the space, or ate the strawberries she'd planted, I thought about her often. In taking over Elsa's plot, I felt that I was in dialogue with her, but also with my nana, a great gardener, who died last autumn.

My nana was the archetypal perfect grandmother: all knitting, all baking, all gardening, aside from being always at the end of the telephone and always delighted to share the highs and lows of my life. As I set about trying to rework the allotment I'd often think "What would nana do?" Probably prune, okay I'll try that then. This allotment has been a cathartic form of grieving for my nana. I've learned a little about vegetables and a lot about my nana in the process.

So now summer's over, I've eaten the last of the raspberries, frozen the rhubarb and the beans, covered the cabbage and sown some onions and garlic (we shall see if they take). It's not as much fun to be up the allotment in the cold! The truth is, I should be up there more than I have been in the past few weeks, what with poor weather and work trips abroad, but just knowing it's there – my space, no one else's – is an amazing gift. I'm not a lover of bracing weather or the rain; but it is a good feeling to know I am responsible for a plot of land, for watching how long vegetables take to grow, for composting more of my house's waste. It's shifted my awareness. I've learned that the more I nurture the plants, the better they are. There's a metaphor there, I'm sure. Nana would be proud!

Busy beehive
Antrim Grove allotment, 2011

SPECIAL PLACES

Antrim Grove allotment in 2011

Belsize Robin
*Photo: D Lawrence*

BELSIZE Remembered

# To our Resurrected Post Office

*Robert Ilson*

**Welcome Home!**

It's good to know our voices have been heard
And once more the typed or hand-written word
Will circulate from here: the little touch
Of personality which means so much
When stamped and mailed to its recipient
That I've performed a simple sacrament
By picking, buying, sticking a stamp on
The envelope that links us in communion.
Let greetings-cards henceforth proliferate
To show we've not forgotten any date
Our friends remember! May "I Love You" stand
Boldly or bashfully in our own hand –
Sent from our own post office back for ever!
(Fight for it!) Frankly, I feared it would never
Return despite our protests. I was wrong:
My dirge transmutes to a triumphal song.
Defeat may well be noble. Victory's better.
I think I'll go off now and post a letter.

Robert Ilson

# Belsize Conservation Areas

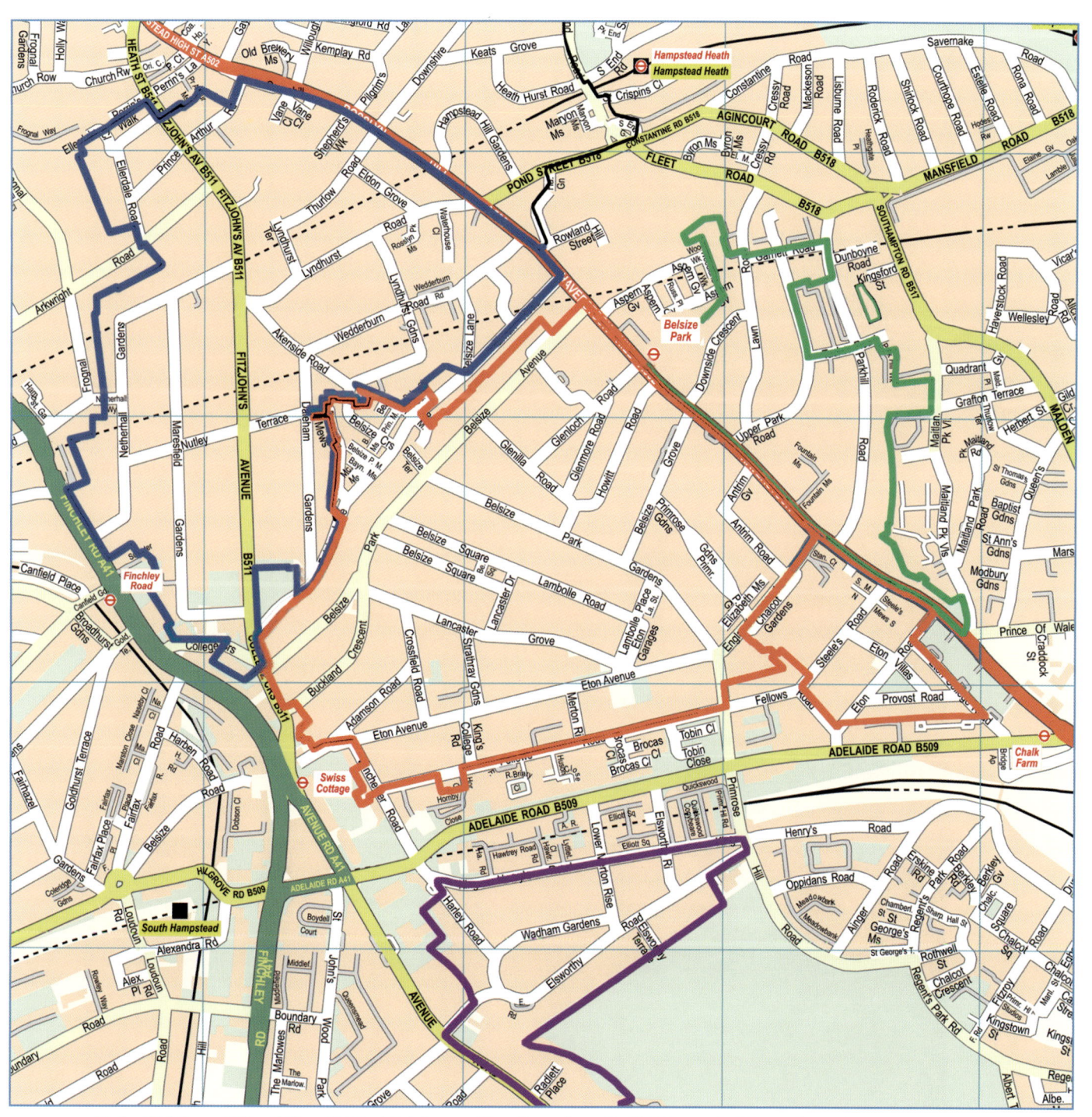

**Central Belsize and Eton College Estate**  **Fitzjohns and Lyndhurst Area**  **Parkhill/Upper Park Area**  **Elsworthy Conservation Area**

BELSIZE Remembered

View towards London from the top of Hampstead Town Hall, Haverstock Hill

Belsize Lane
January 2010

Summer evening in Belsize Village

Stained-glass front door on Glenmore Road

Dusk in Wedderburn Road

# The Belsize Residents' Association

*How the Association helped to preserve the character of the area and develop a stronger sense of community*

The Association grew out of a campaign against a proposal in the early 1970s to build a motorway ring road around Central London, the 'London Motorway Box', which would have swept away swathes of fine Victorian houses in Belsize Park and split Belsize in two. A group of local residents, together with other groups across London, managed to get the scheme dropped. It became clear that a permanent conservation group was needed to fight for the preservation of a district with a unique character. BRA was formally founded in 1976.

One of its early successes brought about the widening of pavements in Belsize Terrace and the addition of trees and benches, turning it from a busy traffic intersection into a peaceful area, the miniature 'Belsize Village', much used as a local meeting place with some attractive pavement cafés.

At first, BRA received many requests for help from young people who became homeless when developers created flats in properties previously used for bedsits. The innovative Belpark Housing Co-operative aimed "to provide affordable housing for local people, in particular to make use of existing buildings which are left empty or allowed to decay". Through Belpark, BRA members worked with squatters occupying 104-110 Haverstock Hill to gain funding to stop these fine houses being demolished and to restore them as good-quality housing for single people.

A formal constitution adopted in 1982 set out BRA's main concerns as:
- Belsize Village improvements
- Pedestrian safety
- Open spaces
- Tree preservation
- Appearance and architecture of new developments
- Forbidding the display of estate agents' boards

By the year 2000 there were 400 members. The 500th household joined at the garden party in 2004, and was rewarded with a bottle of champagne. As the BRA grew, neighbourhood representatives were used to improve communication with members. Local get-togethers were introduced to help members meet others living in the same part of Belsize.

In 1982 BRA started a campaign to eliminate the forests of estate agents' boards from the Belsize Conservation Area. But it was not until 2006, after BRA had agreed to take on the extensive leg work involved in setting up the scheme, that the boards were finally banned.

BRA campaigned in 1987, 1988, 1991 and 2000 to keep the Belsize Library in Antrim Grove open. It remains open, though opening times have been reduced, staffed by doughty volunteers, the Friends of Belsize Library, with whom the BRA continues to work closely.

Despite the efforts of BRA the main post office, and then the sub post office, in Haverstock Hill and the sub post offices in Belsize Village and England's Lane were all closed. In February 2005 the Association organized a march past the site of the original post office in Haverstock Hill to the plaque commemorating Sir Rowland Hill, the founder of the Penny Post. Finally, in 2010 a new sub post office was opened in Thornton's Budgens.

Similar campaigns to save local police stations have met with only partial success, but the fight continues.

Belsize Conservation Area Advisory Committee (BCAAC) was formed at about the same time as BRA and the two organisations work closely together to conserve our historic area. In 1988, after much lobbying, the Belsize Conservation Area was extended to cover the area around Howitt, Glenloch and Glenmore Roads [p179]. Continuous scrutiny of planning applications is a major part of the BRA's workload.

In the late 1980s and 90s a number of significant local buildings were at risk. These included St Stephen's Church,

Lyndhurst Road Congregational Church opposite it, and Hampstead Town Hall. The Congregational Church was purchased and restored to become Air Studios. We were active with other groups in successful campaigns to restore the Town Hall [p97] and St Stephen's [p100] for community use. Our protests about developments at Swiss Cottage, including the loss of the Basil Spence sports centre and the sports pitch, continue with less prospect of success. Campaigns to introduce Article 4 Directions to preserve the distinctive character of the conservation area resulted in their introduction in 2010. The proliferation of basement excavations is a continuing concern throughout London.

Enjoyable architectural walks have over the years covered most aspects of the history of the different estates that make up our area. BRA contributed to decisions about the route for the Belsize Walk that Camden Council introduced in 2005, and financially supported BCAAC in publishing various editions of *Belsize: A Living Suburb*.

From 1973 the BRA organised a Belsize Festival, which included a varied programme of music and other entertainment. This was held in Belsize Village each September, with Belsize Lane closed to traffic. The last festival in 1989 was opened by George Melly and included around 100 stalls. But when, in 1989, wet weather washed out the festival for the third successive year, it dampened enthusiasm for organizing further events.

With the aim of preserving the abundance and rich variety of trees in Belsize BRA established a tree warden scheme and a tree committee. After a particularly dry summer in 1996, when many newly planted trees died, members adopted trees and kept them watered. BRA's most popular event ever was a tree walk in 2004, attended by 130 people. Prizes for well-kept front gardens from 1990 to 2008 promoted the retention of front gardens.

Traffic issues are high on the agenda. After a series of surveys to ascertain local residents' views BRA supported the introduction of parking controls in the north of the area in 1993, the permanent closure of Belsize Terrace to traffic, a 20mph speed limit and improved pedestrian crossings on main roads.

We enjoy good relationships with local councillors of all parties, whilst ensuring that we maintain our non-political status. We also meet with the local police and the Royal Free Hospital about environmental issues.

A regular Newsletter keeps members in touch. In 2003 we set up a website and from 2006 have had a notice board in Belsize Village and since 2011 a second one on Haverstock Hill. Since 1982 members have shared information about tradesmen you can trust. To mark our 40th anniversary we held a survey to find out what our members value about BRA. The highest ratings went to our checking of planning applications, influence on planning policy, contact with councillors, the Newsletters and *Tradesmen You Can Trust*. Members particularly valued the ban on estate agents' boards. They also appreciate opportunities to meet likeminded people and find out more about the area.

So at 40 we are still in good health. But we will no doubt continue to face many challenges in the years ahead as we seek to preserve what is best in Belsize.

**Sources:**
BRA documents held by Camden Local Studies & Archives Centre, 1971-1990
Chapter 'People power in Belsize – does it exist?' by Max Nasatyr and Mary Shenai in *Belsize: A Living Suburb*
Papers of Belsize Conservation Area Advisory Committee, 2010
BRA Newsletters since 1990

BELSIZE Remembered

# Some Notable Former Belsize Residents

Adamson Road 14 - Robert Bevan - artist
Adelaide Road 91 - William De Morgan - ceramic artist
Antrim Mansions 22 - James Agate - drama critic
Avenue Road 81 - Sir Alexander Korda - film producer
Avenue Road, various - Matheson Lang, Marie Tempest
    and Sir Cedric Hardwicke, actors;
    Ludwig and Sir Robert Mond, industrialists
Belsize Avenue 45 - Gordon Harker - actor
Belsize Avenue 56 - Sir James Stirling - architect
Hillfield Court 104 - Diana Wynyard - actor
Belsize Crescent 13 - Berthold Goldschmidt - composer
Belsize Crescent 20 - Twiggy (Lesley Hornby) - model
Belsize House (demolished) - Spencer Perceval -
    later prime minister
Belsize Grove 18 - Sir Richard Rogers - architect
Belsize Park 41 - Jerome K Jerome - novelist
Belsize Park Gardens 6 - Lytton Strachey - artist/critic
Belsize Park Gardens 27 - Henry Brailsford - journalist
Belsize Park Gardens 44 - Frederick Delius - composer
Belsize Square 27 - Miles Malleson - actor
Belsize Square 46 - Hugo Manning - poet
Chalcot Gardens 16 - Arthur Rackham - artist
Downside Crescent 4 - H W Nevinson - essayist
Eldon Grove 1 (Eldon House) - William Dobson - artist
Elsworthy Rd 39 - Sigmund Freud - founder psychoanalysis
Eton Road 2 - R D Laing - psychiatrist
Eton College Road  James Cameron  TV journalist
Eton Villas 1 - Sir John Summerson - architectural historian
Eton Villas 9 - Alfred Stevens - artist
Fellows Road 84 - James Aumonier - artist
Fellows Road 143 - Duncan Grant - artist
Fellows Road 155 - Sir Arnold Bax - composer
Glenloch Road 32 - Alan Ayckbourn - playwright
Glenmore Road 43 - Robert Powell - actor
Haverstock Hill 43 - Stephen Bone - artist
Haverstock Hill 53 - Mark Gertler - artist
Haverstock Hill 145 - Robert Stephenson - railway engineer
Haverstock Hill 160 - William Empson - writer
Haverstock Hill - Phil May - illustrator/cartoonist

King Henry's Road 17 - Elisabeth Lutyens - composer
King Henry's Road 45A - Oscar Kokoschka - artist
Howitt Road 9 - Ramsay Macdonald - prime minister
Lawn Road Isokon building:
    Agatha Christie - novelist
    Marcel Breuer - architect/furniture designer
    Naum Gabo - artist
    Walter Gropius - architect/ founder Bauhaus
    Philip Harben - cook
    Laszlo Moholy-Nagy - artist
    Nicholas Montserrat - novelist
    Adrian Stokes - artist
    Jack Pritchard - furniture designer/builder of Isokon
Lawn Road 84 - John Logie Baird - television pioneer
Lyndhurst Road 6 - Richard Burton - actor
Maresfield Gardens 4 - Cecil Sharp - musician
Maresfield Gardens 20 - Sigmund Freud, Anna Freud
Parkhill Road 7 & 11a - Henry Moore - sculptor and artist
Parkhill Road 54 - Charles Orchardson - artist
Parkhill Road 60 - Piet Mondrian - artist
Parkhill Road Mall Studios:
    George Clausen - artist
    Walter Sickert - artist
    Barbara Hepworth - sculptor
    Ben Nicholson - artist
    Sir Herbert Read - writer and artist
    Sir James Linton  artist
    Robert McBeth - artist
    Cecil Stephenson - artist
Primrose Hill Road 4 - Fred Terry - actor-manager
Primrose Hill Road 8 - Adelina Patti - singer
Primrose Hill Road 32 - Helen Waddell - writer/translator
Steele's Road 31 - Leslie Hutchinson - performer, pianist
Steele's Studios 1 - CRW Nevinson - artist
Steele's Studios - David Bomberg - artist
Steele's Cottage - (now the site of a public house) -
    Sir Richard Steele - dramatist/essayist
Upper Park Road 44 - Thomas Danby - artist
Wedderburn Road 4 - Barry Humphries - actor, comedian

# Author Index

Gene Adams  vii, 64, 78
Ranee Barr  ii, 34
Margaret Beccles  121
Ellie Beutel  166
Paul Birtill  154
Jim Bowen  140
Mona Priwin Wynn Bradley  94, 138
Oggy Boytchev  142
Deborah Buzan  54
James C Cox Jr  126
Tamara Cincik  176
Jean Clarke  28, 172
Dan Carrier  25
Yvonne Deutschman  9
Anthony Dillon  160
Susanna Duncan  48
Bob Enright  168
Barry Ewart  152, 156
Stephany Feher  52
Françoise Findlay  170
Corinne Gibbons  98
Antony Godfrey  90
Anthea Ionides Goldsmith  2
Michael Gorman  86
Celia Greenwood  97
Deepa Gulhane  136
Debbie Bose Harvey  44
Alison Hawkes  32
Isolde Hedegaard  18
Marion Hill  46, 87
Lester Hillman  81
Mayer Hillman  131
Toni Huberman  8
Angela Vandervell Humphery  104
Martin Humphery  104
Eva Ibbotson  4
Robert Ilson  87, 178
Stephen Kahn  149
Tony Kerpel  76
Robert Labi  40, 125, 148
Tim Lamden  84

Helen Marcus  96
Sergio Latorraca  118
Julia Mathews  155
Glenys McDougall  174
Léonie Scott-Matthews  22
Alan Mickelburgh  31
Judith Nasatyr  56, 108, 173
Margaret Nolan  114
Averil Nottage  116
Elizabeth Noyes  74
Margaret Pennell  82
David S Percy  113, 134, 146
Frances Pinter  xv
Piers Plowright  26
Helen Pollock  7, 36, 61, 70, 80
Selom Pomeyie  122
Melanie Price  50
Anna Reiner  4
Marsha Ribeiro  15
Beverley Rice  38
Wendy Richards  66, 162
Michael Roberts  132
Su Rogers  1
Peter Roscoe  88
Darel Seow  112
Priscilla Sharp  102
Janie Shorter  174
Adam Sonin  12
Elaine Joan Spencer  128
Naomi Stadlen  164
Michael Taylor  100
Terry Tidey  158
Nicole Usigli  115
Veronica Jupp Veasey  11, 89
Alfonso Vonscheidt  88
Andrew Welburn  94
June Gibson Williams  110
Anthony Wills  144, 173
Jane Wright
Mel Wright  150
Paul Wright  58

BELSIZE Remembered

# Individual Donors
## Contributors to the Reminiscence Project

Nicola Ansley
Csaba Barta
Dr Raj Barr
Andrew Thornton, Thornton's Budgens
Kate Clark
Ergotec Health Studios
Nick Collins, Hadleigh Residential
Crescent Fruiterers
Deepa Gulhane
Paul Guest
Peter & Elaine Hallgarten
Martin Harcourt
Peter Kadas
Stephen Kahn
Phillips Lavell
Gracian Mariathasan
Marion Mariathasan
Su Rogers & John Miller
Nadia Mitchell
Margaret Pennell
Pomona Foods
Michael & Maria Roberts
Margaret Rudolph
Swans Dry Cleaners
Lajos Varga
The Village Vet
Michael Weatherby
Philip Wood

Chalcot Gardens, artist's window

# Index

## A

Abraxus, The 38
Adams, Gene vii, 64, 78
Adamson Road 8, 20, 34, 39, 40
Adelaide Community Gdns 174
Adelaide Road 83, 166, 170, 174
Aerated Bread Company 170
'A Garden of Eden in Hell' 24
AgeUK 67
air raid shelter 92
air raid Wardens' shelter 40
Akenside Road 126
Alan The Hat 38
Alfresco dining 33
Alidina, Shiraz 9
Allchin & Co 170, 173
Allen, Woody 32
All Hallows 74
All Labour Council 49
Ames House Hostel 129
'A New Neighbourhood' 8
anti-aircraft gun emplacement 74
Antrim Grove 34, 86
Antrim Grove allotment 176
Antrim Road 4, 47, 82, 86
ARP barracks 110
Arrobus, Sydney 119
Art Deco vi, 16, 142, 144
Arts and Crafts Movement 79, 84
Arts Council Lottery Fund 97
Aspern Grove 16, 73, 115, 148
Assn of Jewish Refugees 58
Athill, Diana 48
Auschwitz 26
Austin Motor Co 105
Avengers, The 118
Avenue Road 40
Avoca House Hotel 160

## B

168 bus 144
268 bus 115
Baby Belling 11, 34, 130
baby buggies 32, 39
Bacharach, Evelyn 48
Barlay, Stephen 54
Barnes, Donald 88
barrage balloon 50
Barrett's butchers 168, 173
Barrel House Band, the 150
Barrie, J M 12
Barr, Ranee ii, vii, 34
Bartrams Convent Hostel 68
Bartrams RC convent school 110
Bauhaus 64
Bauhaus-style 90
BBC World Service 142
BCAAC 72, 183
Beatles, The 150
Beccles, Margaret 121
Becoming English 26
bedsits 32, 34, 38
Beecham, Thomas 122
Beechey, Mrs 107
Belleview House 104
bell ringers 66
Belonging 26
Belpark Housing Co-op 182
'Belsize: A Living Suburb' 183
Belsize Avenue 50, 96, 104, 108, 110, 115
Belsize Bookshop xv, 70
Belsize Com Library vii, 46
Belsize Conservation Areas 179
Belsize Crescent 38
Belsize Estate 50
Belsize Festival 38, 56-7, 124, 183
Belsize Fire Station 84
Belsize French Club 46, 87
Belsize Fruit Stores 172
Belsize Grove 1, 4, 16, 24, 34, 40, 52, 74, 83, 123, 134, 143, 166
Belsize House ix
Belsize Lane 2, 38, 39, 58, 110, 134
Belsize Library 46, 82, 86, 149, 183
Belsize Library, Friends of vii, 46, 48, 87, 183
Belsize map 1814 70
Belsize Park Chocolaterie 166
Belsize Park Gardens 4, 15, 26, 34, 38, 40, 102, 125, 128, 132, 134, 139
Belsize Park (road) 8, 20, 39, 44, 160
Belsize Park station 7, 16, 52, 92, 115, 123, 137, 146, 156
Belsize Reminiscence Project vi
Belsize Residents' Association 54, 72, 97, 108, 182-183
Belsize Residents' Newsletter 48
Belsize Square 11, 15, 45
Belsize Square Synagogue 89, 90
Belsize Stores 172
Belsize Tavern, The 31, 38, 115, 118, 149, 150
Belsize Terrace 141
Belsize Village 22, 34, 38, 112, 114, 126, 148
Belsize Village Deli 9, 42, 114
Belsize Festival 38, 123
Belsize Village Post Office 132
Belsize Village rubber stamp 112
Belsize Walk plaques 113
Belsize Woods 72
Bengal 44
Bennett, Alan 48
Bennett, Arnold 12
Benos café 128
Berlin 52, 58, 79
Berlin Mosaic 26
Beutel, Ellie 166
Bevan, Robert 8, 20
Bhagwan Shree Rajneesh 125
bicycles 66
Bieber, Marion 46
Bierkeller, the 130
Birtill, Paul 154
blackout curtains 52
Blakemore, Michael 22
Bliss, Edward xii
Blitz, the 61, 138
Blue-Red Chocolates 166
bohemian 31-32, 54, 86, 142
bohemian market 34
Bombay 15
bombing 52
bomb sites 40
Bond Street 28
Boris Johnson 84
Bose, Bidhan 44
Bose, Meera 44
Bowen, Jim 140
Bowness, Sophie 13
Boytchev, Oggy 142
Bradley, M Priwin-Wynn 94, 138
Bragg, Melvyn 48
'Brain of Britain' 139
breakdance crew 123
Breuer, Marcel 78
Bristow 118
'Britain's Secret Weapon' 88
British Legion 40
British Museum 112
Brynner, Yul 22
Buckland Crescent 20
Budgens 16, 18, 32, 144
Bulgarian secret service 142
Burgh House & Hampstead Museum vii, 17, 65
Burke, David 79
Burtish, Brian 138
Bus conductors 62
Button, Peta 123
Buzan, Deborah 54

## C

Café Flo 16
Camden Council 48, 54, 56, 76, 96, 108
*Camden New Journal* 4, 25, 26, 48, 65

187

Camden Town Group  8
Camomile  35
Canadian Gordon  38
Cannon Place  38
Capri restaurant  128
Carey, Andrew  154
Carrier, Dan  25
Casablanca Club, the  151
Central School of Speech and Drama  40
Chalcots Estate  170
Chalcot Square  15
Chalk Farm  48
Charterton, Roy  48
Chateaubriand  34, 118
Chelmsford Civic Theatre  22
Chez Nous  16, 35, 52, 166
Chicks' Own comic  111
Child, Lauren  87
chocolate shop  34, 166
Christian Community  94, 138
Christie, Agatha  64, 118
Church Commission  115
Church Commissioners  2, 32, 140
Churchill, Winston  79
Cincik, Tamara  176
Circle 33  102
Citri, Oswoldo  31
City & South London Rly  92
C-Jam Blues  150
Clarke, Jean  28, 172
Classic cinema  16, 110, 130, 146
Clayton and Bell  100
clock-mending shop  38
Cluttons  2
Coal hole covers  113
coalman  113
Coates, Wells  78
College Crescent  130, 148
College of Fine Arts  54
Colombo  34
Colour Extensions  18
'Come, Tell Me How You Live'  64
Communism  79
Communist Party Cent Com  142
Compton organ  144
Concrete Crew, the  123

Conrad, Reg  114
Conrad's Bistro  38, 114, 116, 118
Copenhagen patisserie  16
Copperbeech Close  126
Cosmo, The  4, 34, 58
Countess of Chesterfield  ix
Country Club, the  148, 149
Covent Garden  31
Cox, James C Jr  126
Crescent Fruiterers  18, 127
Cressy Road Tram Depot  75
Crouch End  54
Cucina  34
Curtis, Tony  22
Czech Republic  24

## D

Dachau  24
Daleham Gardens  28
Daleham Mews  121
Dallas, TV show  127
Daunt Books  1, 172
D-Day landings  104
'Death Comes as the End'  65
Defoe, Daniel  xi
Delius, Frederick  122
Deutsch, Arnold  79
Deutschman, Yvonne  9
Devil's Dyke  66
Dewhurst butchers  16, 172
Dickens, Frank  118
Dillon, Anthony  160
Dillon, Mary Anne  160
Dillons Hotel  161
Domesday Book  ix
Downshire Hill  23, 83
Downside Crescent  41, 74, 76, 143
Drabble, Margaret  48
Dreyfuss, Richard  81
Dukakis, Olympia  81
Dumb Waiter, The  23
Duncan, Susanna  48
Durga Puja  44-45

## E

East, Alfred  8, 20
East Heath Lodge  2
Edelsten, Anthony  63
Edwards, Gareth  92
Elephant Bill  31
Elizabeth Mews  173
Ellerdale Road  2
Emerson, Ronwen  46
England's Lane  34, 35, 40, 54, 83, 144, 168
English Heritage  84, 92, 100
English Quakers  26
Enright, Bob  168
Eton Avenue  8, 40, 61, 129, 164
Eton College Estate  32
Eton Road  75
Evans, Chris  154
Evans, Eldred  122
Evelyn, John  ix
Everyman cinema  9, 16, 81
Everyman Foyer Gallery  16
Ewart, Barry  152, 156
Exposition Universelle 1889  8
Express Dairy  18

## F

Falafels  116
Fame, Georgie  150
Feher, Stephany  52
Feldman, Marty  129
Fellows Road  8, 40, 144, 174
Fever Hospital  82
Field, Shirley Ann  9
Film: 2001: A Space Odyssey  146
Film: Easy Rider  146
Film: The Graduate  146
Film: 'Last Days, The'  81
Finchley Road  40
Finchley Road and Frognal  130
Finchley Road station  75, 130
Findlay, Françoise  170
Fitzjohn's Avenue  118, 131
Fitzjohn's School  162
Flask, The  9
Fleet Road  74
Fletcher, Dr  75

Ford Motor Co  105
Forsyte Saga, The  42
Fox, Gerry  129
Fraser, Ronnie  154
Frazer, Ronald  31
Freemasons Arms, The  23
Freud, Sigmund  58
Friedrichstrasse  26
Frognal  39, 54
Frugal Sound, the  150
Fuchs, Klaus  79
Fur Clean  38

## G

Galsworthy, John  42
Garner & Pope  148
Garnett Road  82
Garrett Anderson Maternity Home  16, 166
Gauguin  20
Gayhurst Primary School  22
Gent, William  ix
George, The  22, 44, 128
German-Jewish refugees  35
German Jews  90
Germany  26, 58
'Getting On'  49
Gibbons, Corinne  98
Gilbert, Geoffrey  70
Gilling Court  52
Glanville, Stephen  64, 65
Glenilla Road  9, 18, 41, 94, 108, 138
Glenloch Road  22, 31, 138, 170
Glenmore Road  28
Globe Lawn Tennis Club  72
Gmeyner, Anna  4
Godfrey, Antony  90
Gold and Aldridge  86
Golders Green  52
Goldsmith, Anthea Ionides  2
Gorman, Michael  86
goulash  58
Gould, Elizabeth  62
Gould, John  62
Gould, Louisa  62
Gould, Sarah  62
Great Storm, the  61

# INDEX

greenhouses 70
Green, Leslie 92
Greenwood, Celia 97
Grodzinski bakery 16, 128, 172
Gropius, Walter 78
Guildhall School of Music 24
Gulf Wars 142
Gulhane, Deepa 136
Gurney Randall, T 168
Guy Fawkes night 54

## H

Hadleigh Residential 166
Hall Junior School 20
*Ham&High* 4, 13, 48, 58, 94, 102, 104, 115, 162
Hampstead 1, 12, 32, 54
Hampstead Borough Council 96
Hampstead Festival 94
Hampstead Green 68
Hampstead Heath 16, 22, 52, 75, 138, 149
Hampstead Heath station 146
Hampstead Hill Gardens 1, 23
Hampstead Hill School 100
Hampstead Homesteads 102
Hampstead Playhouse 110, 146
Hampstead Register Office 13
Hampstead Theatre 40, 144
Hampstead Town Hall 4, 16, 24, 34, 39, 40, 44, 50, 96, 104, 111, 129, 150, 180
Hampstead Town Hall, Friends of 97
Hampstead Tube 92
Hampstead Vestry Hall 96
Harben Parade 40
Harding, Frank 59
Harvey, Debi 44
Havercourt 52
Haverstock Arms, The 23, 132, 154, 155
Haverstock Hill xii, 1, 16, 22, 32, 34, 35, 36, 40, 70, 142, 149
Haverstock Hill, Nos 104-110, 80
Hawkes, Alison 32
Heath & Hampstead Society 96

Heath Street 23
Hedegaard, Isolde 9, 18
Hedegaard, Peter 18
Hedgecoe, John 7
Hendrix, Jimi 148
Henry VIII ix
Hepworth, Barbara 13, 78
Heritage Lottery Fund 97, 100
Herz-Sommer, Alice 24
Heywoods Estate Agents vii
Hillfield Court 50
Hill House Restaurant 34
Hillman, Mayer 131
Hillman, Lester 81
Hill, Marion 46, 87
Hinchliffe, Sister Judith 174
Hitler 52, 78
Holland, Tony 31
Holmefield Court 16, 52, 166
Holocaust survivor, oldest 24
Holy Trinity Church 130
horse-drawn milk cart 110
Horseshoe, The 23
Housekeeping log book 28
Howard League for Penal Ref 108
Howitt Road 83, 170
HRH the Prince of Wales 97
Huberman, Toni 8
Martin Humphery 104
Angela V Humphrey 104
Hunter, Eileen 162
Hurd, Douglas 61
'Hutch' vi

## I

Ibbotson, Eva 4
'I, Claudius' vi
Ilson, Robert 87, 178
'Inspector Hornleigh Investigates' 139
InterChange 97
Iron Curtain, the 142
Isokon building 64, 78
Isokon Long Chair 65

## J

Jacobi, Sir Derek vi

Jewish Chronicle, The 151
Jewish community 58
Jewish refugees 74
Joachim, Joseph 97
Joan de Normanville Guy 102
John Barnes 50, 148
Jung, Carl xv

## K

Kafka 24
Kahn, Stephen 149
Kalkhof, Peter 18
Kate Greenaway Medal 87
Keats Grove Library 122
Kennedy, Nigel 43
Kerpel, Tony 76
Kerryman, The 160
Kidner, Michael 18
King Alfred School 2
King Henry's Road 170
King's Cross fire 84
Kingsley School 139
Kipling, Rudyard 12
Klooks Kleek club 150
Knocking Shop 121
Kolkata Bengali diaspora 44
Kuczynski, Ursula 79
Kuczynski, Jürgen 79

## L

Labi, Robert 40, 125, 148
La Cage D'Or 148
Lady in Number 6, The 24
Lambert, Catherine 48
Lambolle Place 125
Lambolle Road 54
Lamden, Tim 84
Lancaster Grove 84
landmine 82
Late Late store 18, 124
Late Nite Extra 9, 124
Latorraca, Sergio 118
launderette, Belsize Village 34
Lawn Road 64, 73, 79, 82, 143
Lawn Road Flats 64, 78
Lawrence, D R 73
'Lazy Gardener's Guide' 70

Leapman, Edwina 18
Le Mont, John 150
Le Provençal deli 16
Litvinenko, Alexander 142
Load of Hay, The 144, 152
London County Council 84, 96
London Go Centre 54
London Hostels Association 128, 132
London Motorway Box 182
Lyndhurst Road Congregational Church 88
Lyndhurst Gardens 98, 110

## M

Macdonald, Ramsay 129
Mac Fisheries 40, 74, 170
Macnee, Patrick 118
Maddox, Conroy 32
Ma Durga 44
Mall Studios 12
Manheimer, Marion 58
Manja 4
Mann, Thomas xv
Manor Mansions 134
Manor of Hampstead ix
'Man Without Qualities, The' 26
Marchi-Zeller bakery 125
Marcus, Helen 96
Maresfield Gardens 58, 132
Marie Curie Hospice 46
market gardens 70
Markov, Georgi 142
'Marriage-Go-Round, The' 22
Mathews, Julia 155
Maxwell of Ealing 16
Mayor of Camden 48
McDougall, Glenys 174
McGrath, Joe 123
Measures, Harry 98
Metropolitan line 75
Metropolitan Underground station 20
Michael, George 118
Mickelburgh, Alan 31
Mickey Mouse 138
Miller, Jonathan 48
Milligan, Spike 123

Mini-Concrete Crew 123
Mitchell, Adrian 22
Mondrian, Piet 13
Monty Python 31
Moon and Sixpence café 130, 148
'Moon on the Nile' 65
Moore, Henry 7, 13, 78
Morecambe, Eric 123
'Morning Gift, The' 4
Morris Motors 105
Morris dancers 56
Morris, William 79
Moss, Stirling 105
Mox, The 150
M&S foodhall 16, 110, 146
music man, the 164
'Mysteries', Biber 94

**N**

Nasatyr, Judith 56, 108, 173
Nash, Paul 12
National Lottery 97
Nature for the Community 73
Naval Intelligence USA 126
Nazis 58
Netherhall Gardens 129, 131
Netherhall Way 130, 131
Newcastle-upon-Tyne 52
Newman, Myra vii
News of the World 88
Nicholson, Ben 12, 78
Nicholson, William 12
Nolan, Margaret 9, 114
Northern Line 7, 92
Nottage, Averil 116
Noyes, Elizabeth 74
Nutley Terrace 129

**O**

Oddbins Belsize Village 124, 127
Odeon cinema Haverstock Hill 1, 16, 18, 32, 82, 83, 110, 128, 132, 138, 144
Odeon cinema Swiss Cottage 110
Oliver's Café 9, 38
O'Neil, Daniel ix

Opfer, Felix 26
Orange Prize 87
Ornan Road 104

**P**

Palin, Michael 31
Pancras Square 112
Parkhill Conservation Area 78
Parkhill Road 7, 13, 23, 67, 82, 154, 162
Parkhill Road Studios 82
Parliament Hill 16, 68, 74
Parliament Hill Road 136
Pasmore, Victor 12
Paul, Lynsey de 118
Pears Building, the 101
Pennell, Margaret 82
Pentameters Anthology 23
Pentameters Theatre 23
Pepys, Samuel ix
Perceval, Spencer xii
Percy, David S 9, 63, 113, 134, 146
Peters, Suzi 9
Philby, Kim 79
photocharging 86
Picasso 13
Pilgrim's Lane 12
Pink Floyd 148
Pinter, Frances xv
Pinter, Harold 23
Playgoers Club 22
Playhouse 110
Plowright, Piers 26
Poirot, Hercule 118
Policy and Resources Committee 49
Pollock, Helen 7, 36, 61, 70, 80
Pomeyie, Selom 122
Pond Street 22
Pont-Aven 20
Post House Hotel 39, 44
Post Office 16, 18, 52, 74, 83, 149, 160, 178
Povey, Charles xi
Powell, Robert 154
Prague 24, 52

Premier Inn 110
Price, Melanie 50
Primrose Gardens 34, 113, 136
Primrose Hill vi, ix, 34, 54, 74, 118, 139, 149
'Primrose Hill Remembered' vii
Prince of Wales Road 80
Pritchard, Jack 78
Pryce, Jonathan 38
Pryde, Mabel 12
psychoanalysis 58
Public Library Users Group 46, 48
Pulman, Jack vi
Purple Pussy Cat 130, 148

**Q**

Queen's Silver Jubilee 137

**R**

Rackman, Arthur 31
Radetzky March, The 26
RAF Balloon Command 50
Rafferty, Meryl 158
railway tunnel 72
Rajneesh Centre 54
Ralphs, Dorothy 48
Ram Holder Brothers 150
Randall, Laurie 102
Read, Ernest 170
Read, Herbert 13
Red Sonya 79
Regents Park 149
Reiner, Anna 4
Retracing Ribeiro 16
Ribeiro, Lancelot 15
Ribeiro, Marsha 15
Rice, Beverley 38
Richardson, Dorothy 26
Richardson, Florence 102
Richardson, Spencer 102
Richards, Wendy 66, 162
Riley motorcars 105
Roberts, Michael 132
Roberts, Winifred 13

Robinson, Anne 2
Rocket Gallery 18
Rocque, John ix
Roebuck, The 22
Rogers, Richard 1
Rogers, Su 1
Rolfe, Guy 22
Rolling Stones, The 149
Rosary Primary School 16
Rosary RC School 110
Roscoe, Peter 88
Rosslyn Hill 62, 98, 111, 136
Round House, The 148
Rowland Hill 183
Rowland Hill Street 68, 128
Royal Academy of Music and Drama 22
Royal Free Hospital 68, 100, 122, 129, 184
Royal Society of British Artists 8
Royal Society of Literature 26
Rumbolds bakery 16
Russell, John 72
Russell Nurseries xii, 71, 83, 148
Russell Nurseries Wood 72

**S**

Sainsbury stores 16, 32, 40, 74, 83, 110, 138, 170, 172-3
Saint, Andrew 84
Salmon Florist 71, 83, 132, 146
Salviati of Venice 100
Scarlet, Lt-Col H Ashley- 94, 102
Scotch of St James, The 151
Scott-Matthews, Léonie 22
Screen on the Hill 16, 18, 81, 83
Seow, Darel 112
Servants 62
Shalev, David 122
Sharp, Priscilla 102
'Shelterers in the Tube' 6
Shorter, Janie 174
Siberechts, Jan x
Sickert, Walter 12
'Sigmund Freud's caff' 58
'Simpson & I' 143
Simpson, John 143

# INDEX

Sir Richard Steele, 38, 116, 152
Sisters of Providence 68
Skeaping, Jack 13
Skinner, Ron 151
skip recycling 36
Slade School of Fine Art 12
Sommer, Leopold 24
Sonin, Adam 12, 13
South End Green 16, 22, 50, 143, 147
South End Green Association 96
South Hampstead High School 132
South Hampstead station 139
Spencer, Annie 102
Spencer, Elaine J 128
Spencer House 102
Spencer, Lucy 102
Spies of Lawn Road 78
Spielberg, Steven 81
Sprigge, Annabel 95
SpringHealth leisure club 9, 125
Sri Lanka 34
Stadlen, Naomi 164
stained glass windows 99
Stalin 79
Stanley Gardens 35
Starr, Ringo 118
St Christopher's School 110, 134
Steed, John 118
Steele's Road 38, 62, 144, 153
Steinicke, Eva 26
Stirling, James 1
St Luke's Kentish Town 63
St Margaret's Care Home 174
St Martin's Gospel Oak 66
St Mary's Maternity Hospital 83
St Mary's School, Eton Ave 164
St Pancras 48, 96
St Paul's Primary School 40
St Peter's Church 43, 88, 129
St Peter's vicarage Belsize Square 11, 89
St Saviour's Church 75
St Stephen's Church 34, 74, 88, 100, 110
St Stephen's Preservation Trust 100
St Thomas More Church 132

Suchet, David 118
Summerson, John 174
swimming baths 75
swimming pool 52
Swiss Cottage 25, 34, 40, 58
Swiss Cottage Centre 40
Swiss Cottage Library 18
Swiss Cottage Odeon 144
Swiss Cottage Post Office 132
Sylvia's Sorti Club 121

## T

Taras Bulba 22
Tavistock Centre 58
Taylor, Michael 100
Team 4 Architects 1
Telegraph, The 31
Tennessee Williams 23
Teulon, Samuel Saunders 101
Thatcher, Margaret 129
Theresienstadt 24, 26
Thin Lizzie, rock band 108
Thirlby, Thomas xiv
Thorndike, Sybil 94
Three Horseshoes 23, 129, 151
'Three To Tango' 9
Thurley, Simon 92
Tidey, Daniel xii, 158
Tidey, Terry 158
Times, The 115
Tinkers Folk Club 129
Tiny Tots comic 111
Tivy, Patricia 120
'Toad of Toad Hall' 22
Tootsies 35
Topolski, Feliks 4
Trafford, John 59
Trafford, Ursula 58
Trams 75
Trevor Roberts School 8
Truss, Richard 88
Trust House Forte 105
Tucker, Eva 26
Tudor Close 138
Tunnel Club, The 156
Tushingham, Rita 38
Tuxford, Mrs 110

Twiggy 31, 38

## U

U3A 24, 46, 97
Underground shelter, 7, 92
Unitarian Mission 63
United States 68
University College Hospital 64
University College School 39
Upper Park Road 82, 155
Uryland 28
Ury, Peter 28
Usigli, Nicole 115

## V

Vance, Charles 22
Vandervell, Frank 104
Vandervell, Guy Anthony 105
Vandervell, Percy 104
Vandervell Products 105
Vandervell's Garage 104, 110
Vanwall Formula One 105
Vauxhall Motors 105
Veasey, Veronica Jupp 11, 89
Vicarage, Belsize Square 11, 89
Vienna 40, 58
Village Close 2
Villiers, James 31
Vonscheidt, Alfonso 88

## W

Wac Arts 97
Waitrose 50, 148
Walker, Leonard 170
War Artists' Adv Committee 7
Warden, air raid 40
Warner, Caroline 63
Wartime 40
Washington, The 38, 158, 173
Washington, 'the Wash' 54
Waterloo Bridge 142
Waters, Sarah 87
Welburn, Andrew 94
Werner, Michael 68
Werner, Ruth 79
Westmacott, Mary 64

'When She Comes Back' 26
Whitehorn, Katherine 48
Whitestone pond 16
Wiener schnitzel 4, 58
Willcox, Toyah 9
Willett, William xii, 98
Williams, June Gibson 110
Wills, Anthony 144, 173
Wilson, Kara 9
Winchester Road 40, 56, 164
Winch, the 46, 124, 174
Winmill, Charles Canning 84
Winnie-the-Pooh 48
Witch's Cauldron 22, 38, 114, 115, 116, 148, 149, 150
Woodford, Don xv
Woolf, Henry 23
Woolf, Virginia 26
Wright, Jane 4
Wright, Mel 150
Wright, Miss 110
Wright, Paul 58
World War II xii, 40, 50, 64, 92. 102, 104, 110

## X

XUL Architecture vii

## Y

Ye Olde Swiss Cottage 148
Yiddish 58
Young People's Fellowship 88

## Z

Zimbabwe 143
Zoot Money 150
Zwingli, Madame 11

Images sourced from archive photo libraries:
Camden Local History and Archives Centre, pp. xiii, 14, 25, 30, 168-9, 172 (right)
Historic England, pp. 37, 144-5, 147
London Metropolitan Archives, pp. 85, 158

Visit the **Belsize Village website** for news, photographs, events and information about Belsize Park at **belsizevillage.co.uk**

## The Belsize Story

*The Belsize Story* documentary is narrated by Belsize Park resident Fiona Bruce. Combining its fascinating historical background with a present-day architectural tour, this film records the evolution of Belsize Park right up to the present day, featuring its buildings, the settings and its people. **Free to view online at belsizevillage.co.uk**

Belsize Park residents are welcome to join the **Belsize Residents' Association**
Contact: **membership@belsize.org.uk**